WOODEN TOY PROJECTS

WOODEN TOY PROJECTS

The best from **TOY**MAKING *magazine*

GUILD OF MASTER CRAFTSMAN PUBLICATIONS LTD

This collection first published 1998 by
Guild of Master Craftsman Publications Ltd,
Castle Place, 166 High Street, Lewes, East Sussex BN7 1XU

ISBN 1 86108 097 2

Printed and bound by Kyodo Printing (Singapore) under the supervision
of MRM Graphics, Winslow, Buckinghamshire, UK

Front cover photograph by Dennis Bunn

NOTE

Please note that names, addresses, prices etc. were correct
at the time the articles were originally published, but may
since have changed.

MEASUREMENTS

Throughout the book instances will be found where a metric
measurement has fractionally varying imperial equivalents,
usually within $\frac{1}{16}$in either way. This is because in each particular
case the closest imperial equivalent has been given.
A mixture of metric and imperial measurements should NEVER
be used – always use either one or the other.

CONTENTS

INTRODUCTION

Making wooden toys gives pleasure to so many people, from parents and grandparents to the children themselves – the ultimate recipients of such wonderful playthings.

If you enjoy using tools to breathe life into raw timber, you will certainly enjoy this collection of hands-on projects, selected from the pages of *Toymaking* magazine.

In the sixteen full-colour projects, you will discover a world of movement, sound, colour and laughter. No matter what your interest, there is something for you: ships, trains, planes, mechanical models, games ... there's even a puppet on a string and a boomerang! If you like interactive knock-about toys, why not try your skills at making our ride-on lorry. Go on, give it a whirl.

All projects are based on original designs by the authors, and are supplemented by line drawings, plans and illustrations where required. Step-by-step instructions and relevant cutting lists are also included, to help guide you through all stages of preparation and construction of your chosen toy.

This is a book for enthusiastic toymakers, and includes something to suit all tastes. Fun for all is the name of the game. So get those tools in pristine condition and get busy. Children will have hours of fun playing with your hand-made toys!

Jay Myers
Editor, *Toymaking*

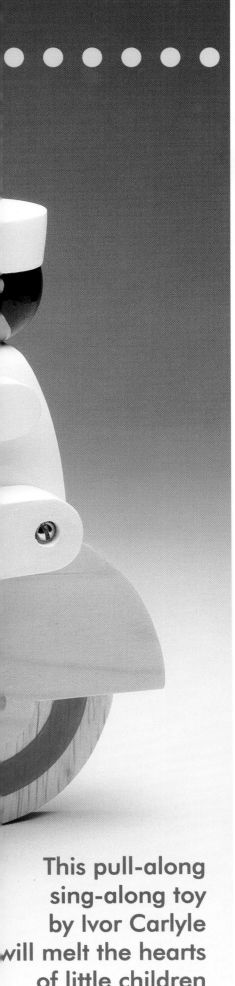

ice cream vendor
music box

My mother-in-law found the remains of a half completed music box at a jumble sale which she presented to me with the comment "I thought you might be able to make something with it".

After throwing away everything, apart from the musical movement, I pondered on how she could have a music box that would entertain her grandchildren and serve as a toy as well. The cycling ice cream seller with his musical chime is the result. He does pedal backwards, but nobody cares.

Cycle/Torso Sections

❶ Start by cutting out and joining together the Cycle/Torso sections,

Materials

12.5mm (½in) prepared pine, in
    120mm (4¾in) width minimum
9mm (⅜in) Plywood
6mm (¼in) Plywood
12.5mm (½in) Hardwood dowel
6mm (¼in) Hardwood dowel
1 x 37mm (1½in) Wooden ball
3 x 12.5mm (½in) Wooden balls
2 x Brass butt hinges and screws
    25mm (1in)
2 x 1½in No 6 Chromed round
    head screws
4 x 9mm (⅜in)Countersink brass
    screws
1 x 21mm (¾in) x No 4 screw
1 x Clockwork musical movement
    with wire stopper
2 x 25mm (1in) Ring key for
    movement
¹⁄₁₆in Brass tube
¹⁄₃₂in Brass rod
PVA woodworking adhesive
Epoxy resin adhesive
1 x 20mm (¾in) Rubber tap washer
Non-toxic coloured enamel and
    transparent lacquer
Small scrap of hardwood
8 x 6mm (¼in) Washers
21mm (¾in) Pine offcuts

front section and rear section. When the glue has set carefully, drill the 6mm (¼in) holes for the pedals' axle and rear wheel axle. In addition, drill 2mm guide holes each side of the body for hip/pivot screws.

❷ With a knife, cut and lift out a groove on one of the box sides to take the brass stopper tube. Also cut out the recesses for the hinges.

Ice Cream Shelf

❶ Fix the support blocks for the ice cream shelf into place on the box sides. Assemble and glue together the Box base sections, box sides, (fit stopper tube and wire before assembling) Front and Back onto the cycle section. Mark the front axle position on the bottom of the box and glue on two 12mm x 6mm (½ x ¼in) strips, leaving a 6mm space between them to hold the axle.

❷ The 6mm (¼in) dowel, that forms the axle, is also glued to the two axle supports. The wheels should run freely on the attached axle, and are retained by 12.5mm (½in) balls at each end. These are drilled to fit the axle and epoxy resin glued on, to retain the wheels.

Thigh Sections

Assemble the outer and inner Thigh sections and drill a 6mm (¼in) hole in the knee joint, but not right through! From the opposite side you have counterbored for the knee drill a 3mm (⅛in) hole in the hip for the pivot screw. Now drill to a depth of 4mm an 8mm (⁵⁄₁₆in) recess to allow the pivot screw head to lie flush with the surface. Remember you need a Right and Left Hand version!

Handlebars

❶ Assemble the Handlebar and stem. Slice a section off the wooden ball to take the hat disc, which should be tapered slightly and glued together. Drill a 6mm (¼in) hole in the base of the head and the top of the Torso.

This pull-along sing-along toy by Ivor Carlyle will melt the hearts of little children

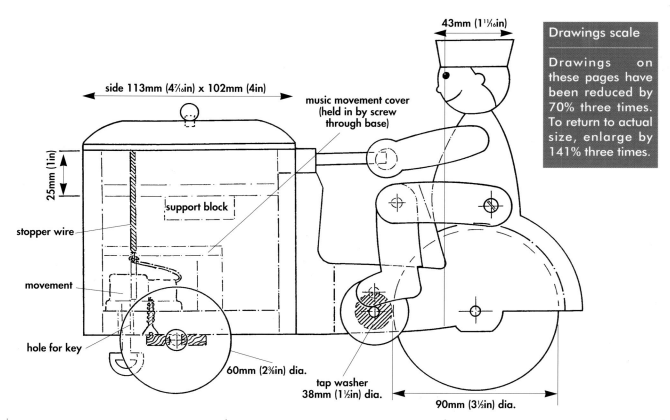

side 113mm (4⅞in) x 102mm (4in)

music movement cover
(held in by screw
through base)

25mm (1in)

stopper wire

movement

hole for key

support block

60mm (2⅜in) dia.

tap washer
38mm (1½in) dia.

43mm (1¹¹⁄₁₆in)

90mm (3½in) dia.

② Counterbore a 12.5mm hole into the hands to take the handlebars. Glue together the movement cover supports and the movement cover.

Finishing

Varnish and paint all the parts before assembling. Counterbore 6mm (¼in)

holes into the 12.5mm wood balls. Resin-glue one of the pedal discs to the dowel axle and push through a washer. Then cycle frame side, insert tap washer between sides and push axle through it and out of the other side. Fit washer and other pedal disc with pedals oppositely opposed.

Rear Wheel

① Fit rear wheel and insert axle rod, not forgetting metal 6mm washers. The rear wheel should rub against the washer and turn the pedals round. It is better to have the rear wheel slightly too tight a fit, and the edge rubbed down, than too small.

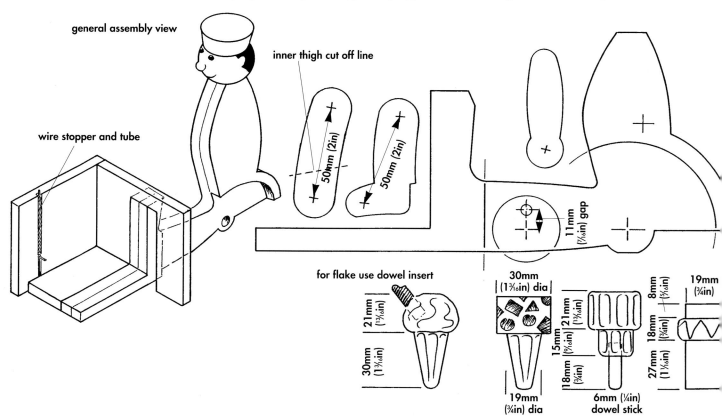

general assembly view

inner thigh cut off line

wire stopper and tube

50mm (2in)

50mm (2in)

11mm (⁷⁄₁₆in) gap

for flake use dowel insert

21mm (¹³⁄₁₆in)

30mm (1³⁄₁₆in)

19mm (¾in) dia

30mm (1³⁄₁₆in) dia

15mm (⁹⁄₁₆in)

18mm (¾in)

21mm (¹³⁄₁₆in)

19mm (¾in)

8mm (¹⁄₁₆in)

18mm (¾in)

27mm (1¹⁄₁₆in)

6mm (¼in) dowel stick

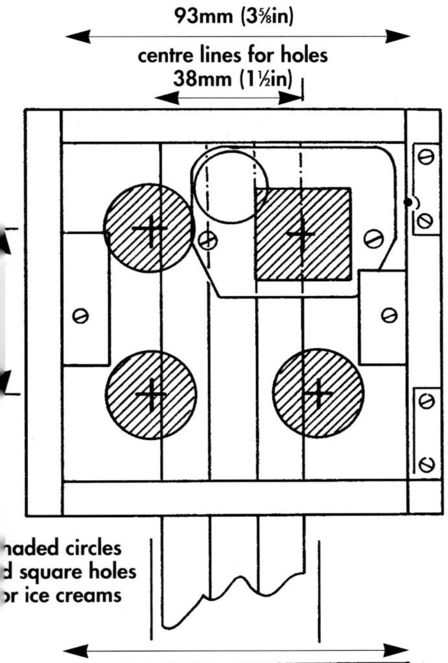

93mm (3⅝in)
centre lines for holes
38mm (1½in)
haded circles
d square holes
or ice creams

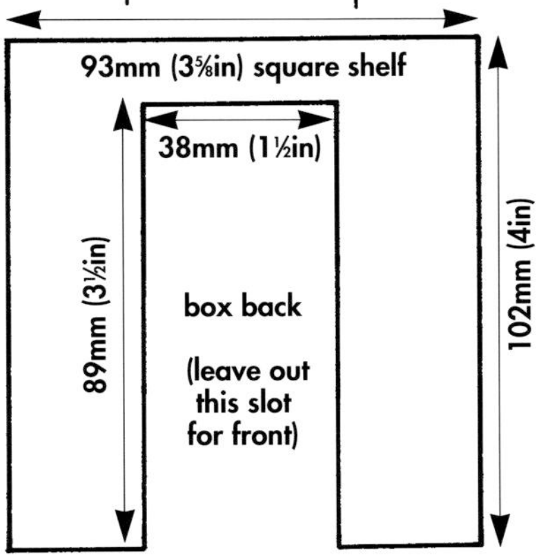

93mm (3⅝in) square shelf
38mm (1½in)
89mm (3½in)
box back
(leave out this slot for front)
102mm (4in)

Insert dowels into the knee joints and fit foot onto pedal and insert screw through hip and washer into Torso.

❷ Use resin adhesive to fix the head, arms, handlebars, front axle, hub caps and box lid ball handle.

❸ Fix the music movement cover with a screw inserted through from the base, followed by the Ice cream shelf which is held in by two screws onto the support blocks.

The musical movements are available from hobby and craft shops as well as mail order companies such as Hobbies, Dereham, Craft Supplies, Derbyshire and W. Hobby, London. ●

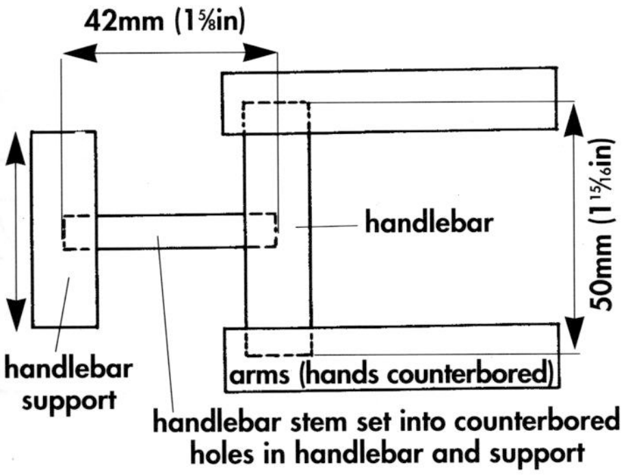

42mm (1⅝in)
handlebar
50mm (1 15/16in)
handlebar support
arms (hands counterbored)
handlebar stem set into counterbored holes in handlebar and support

Cutting list

12.5mm (½in) Pine
2 x Cycle/Torso sections 256 x 121mm (10 1/16 x 4¾in)
1 x Cycle front section 122 x 87mm (4¾ x 3 7/16in)
1 x Cycle/Torso section (rear) 110 x 80mm (4 5/16 x 3⅛in)
2 x Arms 67 x 20mm (2⅝ x 13/16in)
1 x Hat 43mm (1 11/16in) Dia.
2 x Front wheels 60mm (2⅜in) Dia.
1 x Support block 12 x 36mm (7/16 x 1⅜in)
1 x Support block 12 x 26mm (7/16 x 1in)
1 x Box lid 112 x 112mm (4⅜ x 4⅜in)
1 x Movement cover support 70 x 30mm (2¾ x 1 3/16in)
1 x Movement cover support 51 x 30mm (2 x 1 3/16in)
2 x Box base sections 27 x 93mm (1 1/16 x 3 11/16in)

21mm (¾in) Pine
4 x Ice creams 51 x 30mm (2 x 1 3/16in)

9mm (⅜in) Plywood
2 x Box sides 112 x 102mm (4⅜ x 4in)
1 x Box front 93 x 102mm (3⅝ x 4in)
1 x Box back 93 x 102mm (3⅝ x 4in)
1 x Rear wheel 90mm (3½in) Dia

6mm (¼in) Plywood
4 x Outer thigh sections 72 x 24mm (2 13/16 x 15/16in)
2 x Inner thigh sections 51 x 24mm (2 x 15/16in)
2 x Leg and foot sections 65 x 37mm (2 9/16 x 1 7/16in)
2 x Pedal discs 38mm (1½in) Dia.
2 x Axle supports 111 x 14mm (4⅜ x 9/16in)
1 x Music movement cover 70 x 62mm (2¾ x 2 7/16in)
1 x Ice cream shelf 93 x 93mm (3 11/16 x 3 11/16in)

12.5mm (½in) dowel
1 x Handlebar 50mm (2in)

6mm (¼in) dowel
1 x Lolly stick 25mm (1in)
1 x Handlebar stem 42mm (1 11/16in)
1 x Rear axle wheel 38mm (1½in)
1 x Pedal axle 50mm (2in)
2 x Pedals 12mm (½in)
1 x Front axle 146mm (5¾in)
2 x Knee axles 16mm (⅝in)
1 x Nose 9mm (⅜in)
1 x Neck joint 21mm (13/16in)

Hardwood offcut
1 x Handlebar support 38 x 12 x 12mm (1½ x ½ x ½in)

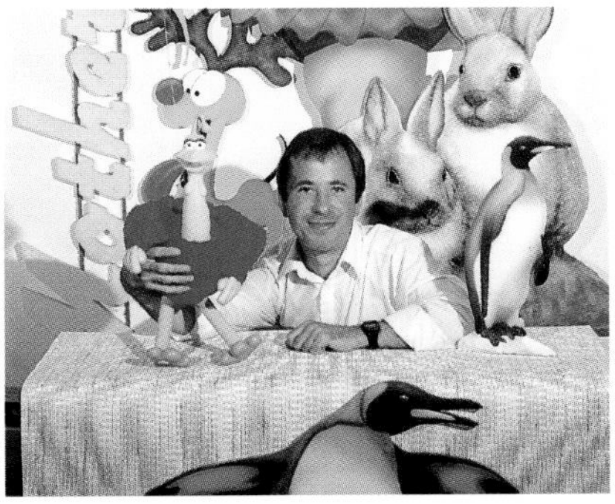

Ivor Carlyle works full time as an illustrator and model maker, covering diverse subjects such as a Working Model Watermill to Puppet heads and Props for Advertising photography. An increasing number of nephews and nieces prompted an interest in producing quick and easy-to-make toys.

DIZZY DUCK

A duck, designed and made by Jeff Loader, comes in for some rough treatment from the children. Hence the name

Dizzy, the push-along duck, is so called because of the way in which my children play with him. They zoom him around the living room carpet, hurtle him up the stairs and drive him over their beds. What duck wouldn't get dizzy with such treatment?

Operated at a more sedate pace, the alternate movement of each foot enables Dizzy to gently waddle from side to side.

Construction

❶ Transfer the duck profile onto 18mm, ¾in MDF or birch plywood. Ensure that you mark the axle hole centre and the control rod centre line.
❷ Cut the profile out with a powered fretsaw. You will find a size 11 blade suitable. If you do not have access to a powered fretsaw, you could carefully use a coping saw as an alternative.
❸ Drill the axle hole to allow the

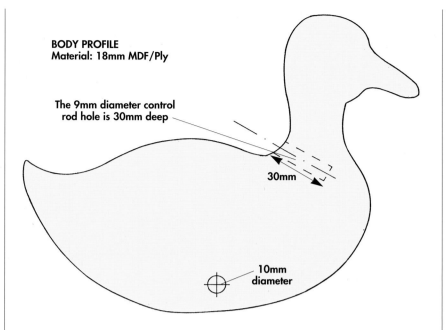

BODY PROFILE
Material: 18mm MDF/Ply

The 9mm diameter control
rod hole is 30mm deep

30mm

10mm
diameter

Materials

Duck body (1)
    225 x 175 x 18mm, 8⅞ x 6⅞ x
    ¾in MDF or birch plywood
Control rod (1)
    500 x 9mm, 19¹¹⁄₁₆ x ⅜in
    hardwood dowel
Handle (1)
    25mm, 1in hardwood ball
Axle (1)
    47 x 9mm, 1⅞x ⅜in
    hardwood dowel
Wheels (2)
    60 x 12mm, 2⅜ x ½in birch
    plywood or MDF discs
Feet (2)
    50 x 26mm, 2 x 1½in orange
    or yellow felt
Washers (2)
    M10 zinc plated or brass

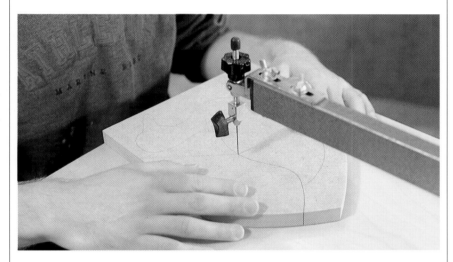

9mm diameter dowel to turn freely when placed into it. I found a 10mm diameter drill bit to be ideal.

④ Drill the hole to take the 9mm dowel control rod. To do this clamp the duck in a vice so that the marked centre line is vertical. Use a try square, placed on the outer jaw of the vice, to aid you. Now drill the hole 30mm, 1³⁄₁₆in deep. A simple depth indicator can be made by wrapping adhesive tape around your drill bit 30mm, 1³⁄₁₆in from the cutting end.

TIP 1 Doweling, whatever the diameter, rarely comes in the exact size it purports to be. For example, 9mm is invariably a fraction over 9mm in diameter. Therefore, it is advisable to obtain a selection of drill bits sized 9mm and around – such as ⅜in, 9.5mm and even 10mm.

Above **Cutting out the duck body from 18mm MDF**
Below **Drilling the control rod hole. Note the tape wrapped around the drill bit as a depth indicator**

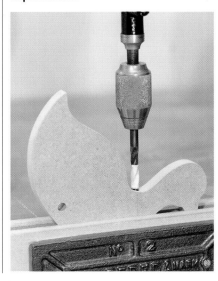

(*If you haven't a selection of drills to provide the correct dimension for an easy dowel fit, use of abrasive paper at the 'business end' of the dowel will remedy the problem.* – Ed)

TIP 2 Always test the suitability of the drill bit size prior to drilling into your work piece. Drill a test hole into a piece of scrap material. Check that your doweling fits correctly. If not, select another drill bit size and repeat the test until the correct size is found.

⑤ Thoroughly sand the duck all over. The edges should be lightly rounded over.
⑥ Sand smooth a length of 9mm doweling and cut a 500mm, 19¹¹⁄₁₆in length. This will be used for the control rod.
⑦ Drill a 9mm diameter hole, or whatever size ensures that the dowel control rod fits snugly, halfway into a 25mm, 1in diameter hardwood ball.
⑧ Glue the hardwood ball onto one end of the control rod.
⑨ Mark out two 60mm, 2⅜in diameter circles onto 12mm, ½in birch plywood or MDF using a compass. These will be the Dizzy's wheels. (*Alternatively, wheels can be turned on a lathe or even produced on the drill press or horizontally-held power drill.* – Ed)
⑩ Mark the foot slot onto each wheel.
⑪ Drill out the centre of each wheel

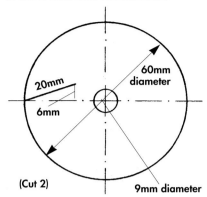

WHEEL
12mm birch plywood/ MDF
The foot slot is 20mm deep.
Its end is 6mm from the centre line.

20mm

6mm

60mm diameter

9mm diameter

(Cut 2)

to accept the 9mm doweling axle.

⑫ Cut out each wheel. A no. 5 grade blade is ideal if using a powered fretsaw.

⑬ Cut the foot slots in each wheel. I cut them progressively – fretsaw first, then tenon saw, finishing with an 8 t.p.i. crosscut saw. In this way I found that the surface ply grain is less likely to split out. The crosscut saw also provided a snug fit for the feet.

(*An alternative approach to using three saws – and to enable a splinter-free cut – would be to score the surface both sides, where the cut is required, with a sharp knife. Also self adhesive tape applied to the underside is a further means of avoiding splintering. – Ed*)

⑭ Cut the axle from 9mm dowel. A 47mm length should suffice, but

Cutting the foot slot in a wheel using a crosscut saw

check before you cut.

⑮ Thoroughly sand the wheels and fix the axle into one of them using wood glue.

⑯ Paint the duck and wheels to a colour scheme of your choice. I used Humbrol Enamel paint, Gloss White (No. 22); Gloss Tan (9); Gloss Midnight Blue (15); Gloss Yellow (69) and Gloss Black (21).

⑰ Varnish the control rod.

TIP 3 Finishing is made easier by using a simple jig. This can be nothing more complex than a wooden block with holes drilled into it to accommodate the various components. Offcuts of dowel can be used to support the duck and the wheel without the axle attached.

All the components prior to finishing and assembly

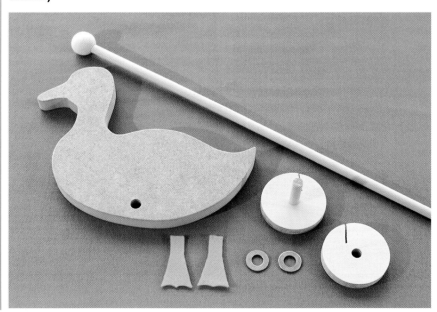

⑱ Glue the control rod into position.

⑲ Transfer the foot profile onto a piece of card and cut it out. This will be used as a template.

⑳ Place the template onto a piece of orange or yellow felt and mark around it with a pen. Do this twice.

㉑ Cut out each foot with sharp scissors.

FOOT

Felt (cut 2)

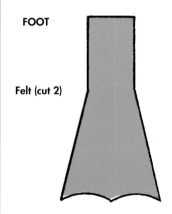

㉒ Slide each foot into the slots on the wheels, using a small thin bladed screw driver to aid you. Fix each foot in place with a spot of glue if necessary.

㉓ Add the M10 washer to the axle (dowel) which has previously been

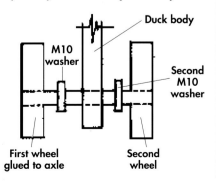

Duck body

M10 washer

Second M10 washer

First wheel glued to axle

Second wheel

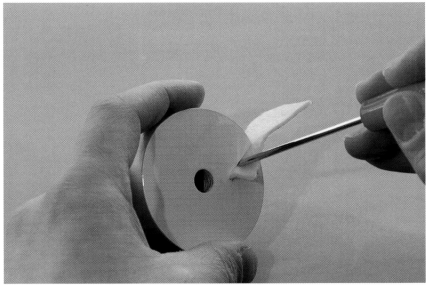

Top **Painting jig**
Above **Fitting a foot**
Right **Dizzy Duck and Sam**

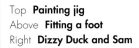

glued to the first wheel. Then pass the axle through the hole previously drilled in the duck's body, then add the second washer and finally glue on the second wheel. Ensure that the foot slots of the wheels are opposing each other. This is so that when one is at its uppermost position, the other is at its lowest. This will ensure that Dizzy waddles correctly.

24 Finally, touch in the exposed axle end with paint. ●

Jeff Loader's woodworking career led him to set up and run a wooden toymaking workshop. This not only involved design and manufacture, but also the instruction of novices in various workshop practices and methods. Through this work he soon realised the love and joy of making, and playing with, wooden toys.

Jeff has written articles for various woodworking and modelling publications, as well as co-writing Making Board, Peg and Dice Games (GMC Publications Ltd) with his partner, Jennie.

Wooden toys and games apart, Jeff's many interests and activities include furniture design, restoring and using old woodworking tools, sport and playing (coping!) with his young family.

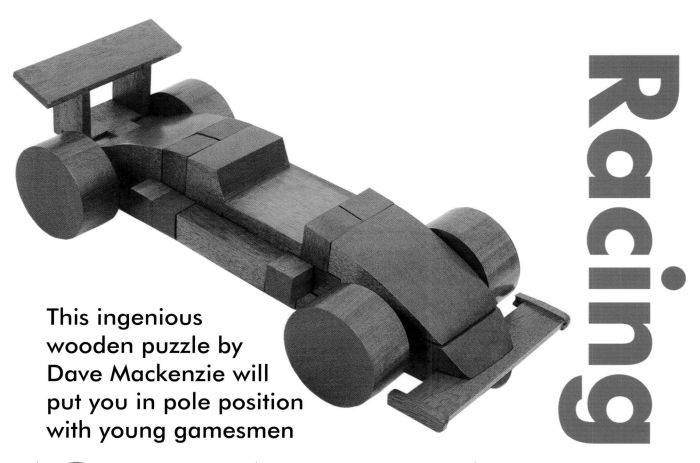

Racing car puzzle

This ingenious wooden puzzle by Dave Mackenzie will put you in pole position with young gamesmen

This interlocking puzzle is relatively simple to make but requires care to ensure the parts fit together accurately. Although It can be made from any wood, best results will be obtained if straight grained pieces of hardwood are used. Allow 25 hours from start to finish for its construction.

To mark out the pieces you need a rule, a marking gauge, a try square and a marking knife. All of the pieces can be cut out using a tenon saw, a coping saw, a bevel edged chisel and a plane.

A router with a straight cutter is very useful for making notches to a constant depth in all of the pieces – particularly on the three large body sections – but it is not essential; use a square file to smooth the base of the grooves if a router is not available.

To make the wheels, use a lathe or cut out suitable disks using a hole-cutting saw fitted to a power drill. Access to a bandsaw and a sanding disc makes shaping the profile of some of the pieces an easier task.

Scale drawings

The dimensions of the pieces are based on a single square unit. The size of the puzzle depends on the size selected for this unit. One square

in the drawings represents one unit. My car has a unit size of 9 by 9mm, ⅜ by ⅜in. If a smaller unit size is selected then the model will be smaller.

Selecting a unit size of 9mm, ⅜in results in a puzzle that is about 305mm, 12in long.

'Master' pieces

Before starting, make a couple of 'master' pieces. These are not part of the puzzle, but are used as accurate gauges from which all the notches in the actual puzzle pieces are marked. This will give better results than trying to measure the unit size on each individual piece.

These 'master' pieces are short lengths of 2 by 2 square units and 1 by 2 units. Plane them so that the corners are exactly square. Time will be saved later if trouble is taken to ensure that these are as accurate as possible.

Construction

❶ Starting with the smaller square sectioned pieces shown on Drawing B, pictures 1, 2, 3, and 4, **see photo 1**, cut a length, long enough for all of them, and plane it square with the two sides exactly the same width.

Drawing A   each square represents a unit

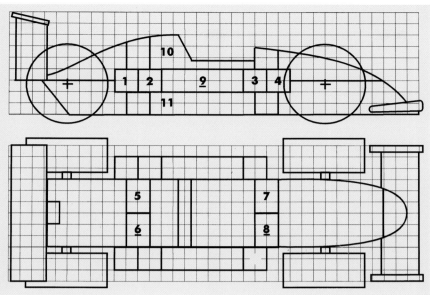

**Drawing B
The 2 x 2 square section
units (1,2,3,4)**

This is a 1 x 1 unit
square notch

This is a 1 x 1 unit
square notch

Ensure that the pieces are marked with the identification letter in the correct orientation. This will make them easy to fit together with reference to the solution drawings

Photo 1 **Smaller square sectioned pieces 1, 2, 3 and 4.**

❷ To make the first piece, cut the prepared square sections to length, mark off where the first notch is to be cut, using the 'master pieces', **see photo 2**, and then use a 'master piece' to achieve the width of the notch.

❸ Mark the sides of this with a try square, **see photo 3**. Indicate the waste areas with cross-hatching and mark the depth of the notch with a marking gauge, **see photo 4**. Cut the sides with a tenon saw, **see photo 5**, and clean out the waste with a chisel, **see photo 6**. Make all of the pieces in a similar way.

❹ Pieces 3 and 4 each have a notch that is a single unit. These are made by cutting across the corner with a tenon saw, as far as is possible, and then forming the notch with a bevel edged chisel.

Adjustments

❶ When the notches are cut, test them to see if they are the correct width and depth with the master pieces, **see photo 7**, and make any adjustments required. The fit should not be so tight that they have to be forced together, and not so loose that the master pieces will wobble in the notches. Ideally they should slide smoothly. Use combinations of pieces to test the holes that are wider than one or two units.

❷ As each piece is made, mark the identification letters on the ends, in the same position and orientation as the drawings. With the aid of the solution, **see panel**, this will enable the pieces to be fitted together quickly as work proceeds, so that the fit can be adjusted.

Photo 2 Marking off where the first notch is to be cut, using the 'master' piece.

Photo 3 Marking the sides of the 'master' piece with a try square.

Photo 4 Marking the depth of the notch with a try square.

From top to bottom
Photo 5 **Cutting the sides with a tenon saw.**
Photo 6 **Cleaning out the waste with a chisel.**
Photo 7 **Testing the cut notches for width and depth, using the 'master' piece.**
Photo 8 **Pieces 5, 6 7 and 8.**

Drawing C

The 3 x 2 square section units (5,6,7,8)
The pieces are drawn from the viewpoint that shows the various cuts and notches best
Ensure that the pieces are marked with the identification letter in the correct orientation. This will make them easy to fit together with reference to the solution drawings

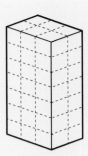

Blank piece showing unit section size. They can all be cut from a piece this size

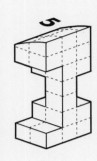
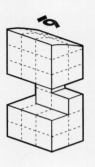
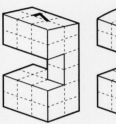
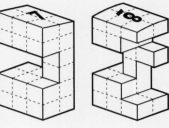

Test for fit

❶ Pieces 5,6,7,8, shown on Drawing C, **see photo 8**, are made next in a similar way to the square pieces. When pieces 1,2,5,6 and pieces 3,4,7,8 are cut, try putting them together to test that they all fit. Pieces 5,6,7,8, are dissimilar in length although the section size (3 by 2 units) is common to all four.

❷ The variation in the length is due to the shape of the top of the car. When cutting the length, do not attempt at this stage to shape the top profile, but simply leave enough wood to allow the tops of the pieces to be shaped after the body sections have been finished.

❸ Start measuring the position of the notches from the bottom end of the pieces because they are flat at this end.

Complex sections

❶ The three main body sections 9,10,11 shown on Drawing D, E, F, G, **see photos 9 and 10**, are the most complex but, after practising on the simpler parts they should not present too much difficulty, as the basic techniques used to produce them are the same.

❷ When I made my model I used a router to ensure all the grooves were a constant depth.

❸ A coping saw, or, better still, a bandsaw, can be used to shape the curves on the top of the top body section and the front of the lower body section; the curves can then be filed smooth.

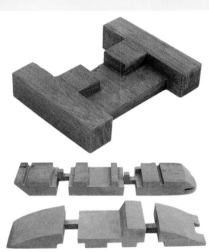

Photos 9 and 10 **The three main body sections 9, 10 and 11 are the most complex.**

Top profiles

❶ The top profiles of pieces 5,6,7,8 are drawn and then cut after fitting them in place into the shaped body.

❷ Make the grooves that house the axles in the lower body section; I used a router fitted with a half round cutter for this, but an alternative method would be to use a tenon saw to cut the sides, and a small diameter round file to form the shape at the base of the groove.

Rear spoiler

❶ The rear spoiler shown on Drawing H, **see photo 11**, is fixed to a long piece of the puzzle; the spoiler is inserted through the middle section of the car, so locking all the other pieces into place.

❷ This long locking piece must be made as accurately as all the other

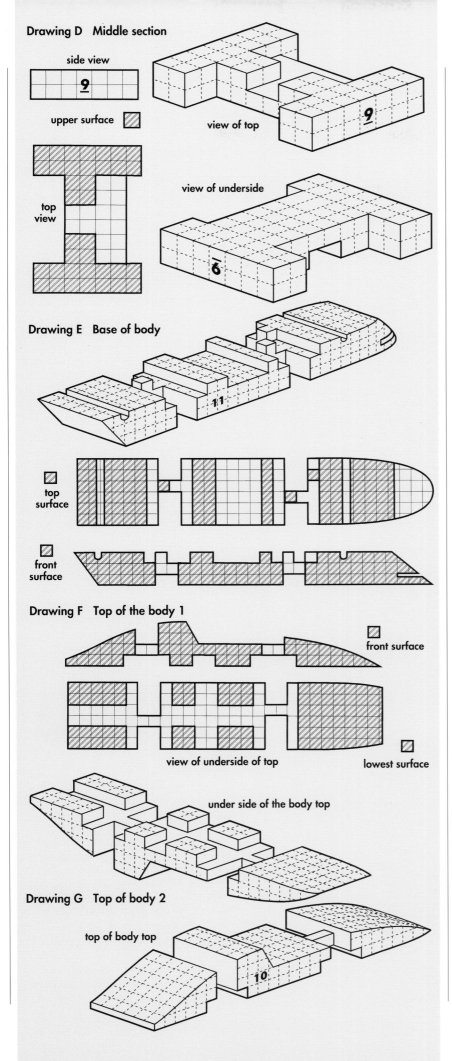

Drawing D Middle section

side view

9

upper surface

view of top

9

top view

view of underside

6

Drawing E Base of body

11

top surface

front surface

Drawing F Top of the body 1

front surface

view of underside of top

lowest surface

Drawing G Top of body 2

under side of the body top

top of body top

10

Photo 11 **The rear and front spoilers.**

body parts, but the size and shape of the spoiler does not have to be as accurate, and there is scope for individual creativity. I chose to join the spoiler's vertical sides to the base using box joints; and housing joints are used to fix the top of the spoiler to the sides.

3 A tenon saw and a 6.35mm, ¼in and 3.2mm, ⅛in chisel are used for making these joints. The spoiler is joined to the locking piece with a glued halving joint.

Front spoiler

1 The front spoiler shown in Drawing I is a slice of wood about half a unit thick, which has two square sections with rounded corners fitted to the ends with housing joints.

2 To make these small joints, cut the sides of the end piece housings with a marking knife and chisel out the waste. They are held in place with glue. When they are fixed into place, round the corners with glass-paper for a realistic appearance.

3 A slot is cut in the base of the body, piece 11, for the front spoiler to fit into.

Making the wheels

1 The wheels, **see photo 12**, are discs of wood connected with 6.35mm, ¼in hardwood dowelling that is fitted into holes drilled in the centres. To make them on a lathe,

Photo 12 **The wheels.**

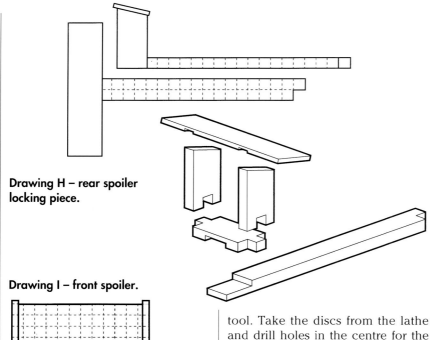

Drawing H – rear spoiler locking piece.

Drawing I – front spoiler.

turn a cylinder to the correct diameter and then separate it into individual wheels using a parting tool. Take the discs from the lathe and drill holes in the centre for the axles.

② Ensure that the drill holes are 90° to the surface of the disc and do not drill completely through the wood, particularly if the hardwood used for the wheels is a different type or colour to that used for the axles.

③ If the wheel discs are made using a hole saw, then there might be holes drilled completely through the disc. The finished wheels will look better if these holes are plugged on the outside with a hardwood plug made from the same type of wood as the wheels, so that it does not show.

Assembly

① Assemble the body section, and shape the rounded front of the car with a coping saw followed by a file. A disc sander is excellent for achieving a good final finish, and should be used after the puzzle has been assembled, so that all the pieces are flush with the surface. For some of the sanding stages, leave out pieces that protrude, so that the sides can be smoothed in one piece.

Finish

① I used a single coat of matt polyurethane varnish followed by wax polish.

② If the pieces have been made accurately, several coats of varnish will build up the thickness and might cause them to bind together.

③ After a single coat has been applied, rub the pieces down with steel wool and follow this with several applications of furniture wax. This will not only make it look good, it will also help the pieces to slide in a satisfactory way. ●

Solution to puzzle

Group together 1, 2, 5, 6, and 3, 4, 7, 8 as shown, with a gap of 1 unit between the vertical pieces 5, 6 and 7, 8.
Put them in position in lower body 11, but do not close them up.
Put 9 and both sets of wheels into place.
Lower the top into position and close up pieces 5, 6 and 7, 8.
Slide the front and back spoiler into the slots and it's done.

Solution to puzzle.

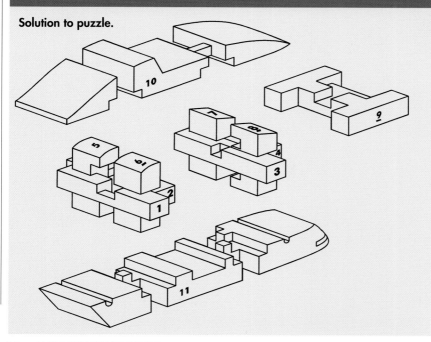

Since giving up his day job in the electronics pre-press industry, Dave Mackenzie now divides his time between lecturing – on graphic design, DTP and magazine journalism – and woodworking.
He has had a couple of hundred magazine articles on woodworking and DIY published over the last 20 years. These articles range from furniture design to kite making and much else in between. His first book, *Making Pine Furniture Projects*, will be published by GMC Publications Ltd in April this year.
Dave Mackenzie is married with two children and enjoys painting, walking and twitching.

Tractor and Log Trailer

Inside the house or out in the garden, children will have plenty of fun playing with this simple vehicle designed by Glyn Salisbury

Whenever I design a new wooden toy I adhere to three principles:

1) There is no metal used in the construction if possible.

2) Do not paint everything if an item is made in wood. By all means add a little colour, but do not hide the wood.

3) Do not make a toy so complex that there is no room for a child's natural imagination.

Tools and accessories required are a saw, disc sander (the most popular for any shed is a small bench-mounted version powered by an electric drill), glue, varnish and your own imagination.

You can use hardwood if you wish, but pine is quite adequate for most children's rough play. All timber, doweling, glue and finishes can be purchased from you local timber merchant or hardware shop; 75mm x 25mm (3in x 1in) is used in the main. For the tractor engine and cab you may even have a few offcuts to use.

Cutting list

Pine Stock
75mm x 25mm (3in x 1in) x 990mm (39in)
50mm x 50mm (2in x 2in) x 90mm (3½in)
75mm x 50mm (3in x 2in) x 100mm (4in)

Hardwood strip
6mm (¼in) x 32mm (1¼in) x 113mm (4½in)

Doweling
9mm (⅜in) x 660mm (26in)
6mm (¼in) x 127mm (5in)
Various sizes for logs (i.e. broom handle)

The sturdy-looking tractor engine and cab.

The Engine

1 Mark and square off a section of pine 50mm x 50mm (2in x 2in) by 19mm (3¼in) long (*figure 1*). Once sawn to length sand all faces until everything is square. Select the two faces you prefer for the front and the top.

2 On the top face mark a spot 13mm (½in) in from the side and the front.

3 Using a 9mm (⅜in) bit, drill a hole 19mm (¾in) deep.

4 Except for the edges around the bottom and back faces sand a heavy 6mm (¼in) radius on all remaining edges. The two upper corners on the front will require blending in.

5 Cut a 50mm (2in) length of 9mm (⅜in) dowel, chamfer both ends and glue into the drilled hole. A pin hammer may be needed if it's a tight fit.

Fig 1   Tractor engine block

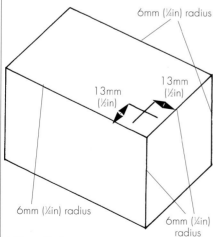

6mm (¼in) radius

13mm (½in)

13mm (½in)

6mm (¼in) radius

6mm (¼in) radius

The Cab

1 From a length of 75mm x 50mm (3in x 2in), mark, square and cut off a piece 83mm (3¼in) long (*figure 2*). Sand all faces until the block is square. Select the face you prefer to be the front and the top.

Fig 2   Tractor cab

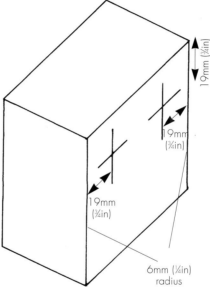

19mm (¾in)

19mm (⅜in)

19mm (¾in)

6mm (¼in) radius

2 From the top, mark a line 19mm (¾in) down. Coming in from both sides, mark a spot 19mm (¾in) in; use a 25mm (1in) borer to bore straight through. These are the windows and care should be taken when the bit breaks through. The two leading edges of the cab need a radius to match the engine. Then, using 100 grit sandpaper around your finger,

work a heavy radius on the entry and exit edges of the windows.

3 Apply a light coat of wood glue to the rear face of the engine. Place both engine and cab on a flat surface and press glued face to front of cab, centralising by line of sight. Set aside to dry.

4 The roof of the cab measures 75mm x 25mm (3in x 1in) and should match the width of the cab. Sand all round until square. Curve all corners to an approximate 13mm (½in) radius.

5 Apply a light layer of glue to the top of the cab and press on the roof, aligning the sides of roof with the sides of cab. Ensure there is an equal overhang to front and rear.

Tractor base

This comprises two sections of 75mm x 25mm (3in x 1in). One is 200mm (8in) long. The second is 38mm (1½in) long.

1 Cut both pieces and sand square all round. The rear of the base needs to be angled off. Each angle is 38mm (1½in) down the sides and 22mm (⅞in) in towards the centre line (*figure 3*).

Fig 3

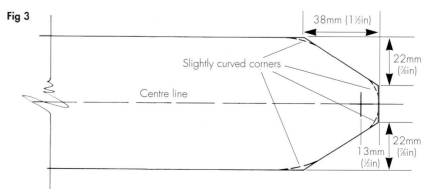

38mm (1½in)

22mm (⅞in)

Slightly curved corners

Centre line

13mm (½in)

22mm (⅞in)

② Mark the centre line and from the end measure 13mm (½in). At this spot drill a 9mm (⅜in) hole, 13mm (½in) deep. Cut off the angles and re-sand. Curve the shallow angles and slightly round off the narrow centre section. Cut a 41mm (1⅝in) length of 9mm (⅜in) dowel. Chamfer both ends and glue into hole. This is the tow-hitch.

③ Measure and mark the axle hole (*figure 4*). When drilling the axle hole use an 8mm (⁵⁄₁₆in) drill and hold the axle block against a larger square offcut. You can also use a clamp or a small machine vice. Once drilled put a 3mm (⅛in) chamfer on all the bottom edges. Slightly blend in by hand sanding.

Fig 4   Tractor axle block

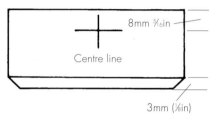

④ Glue the block into position, 13mm (½in) back from the leading edge of the base. Use a square against the side of the base to ensure correct alignment.

⑤ With the base upside down take the time to cut off a piece of the hardwood strip, 113mm (4½in) long. Bevel all endgrain edges. Apply glue to the leading face of the base and press bumper into position. Centralise to ensure an equal overhang either side. Set the assembly aside to dry.

Trailer

The trailer base is a 229mm (9in) length of 75mm x 25mm (3in x 1in).

① Once sawn off, sand square all round. The front has identical angles to the cab base (*figure 3*).

② The spot marked for the towing hitch is drilled through with a 13mm (½in) bit. When sanding the angle the appearance is enhanced if you sand a 13mm (½in) radius on the rear corners of the trailer. The axle block is almost the same as the tractor axle block.

③ Measure for the axle hole (*figure 5*) and drill a hole using a 13mm (½in) bit. Locate the centre of the block by drawing lines diagonally from corner to corner. As you are using a larger

Plenty of room in the trailer; why not add some sawn-off branches too?

drill bit I suggest you either clamp or use a vice.

Fig 5   Trailer axle block

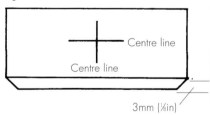

④ When complete and sanded it can be glued into place, 25mm (1in) in from the rear edge. Set aside for a while.

⑤ For the log supports cut off two lengths of 29mm (1⅛in) from the remainder of the 75mm x 25mm (3in x 1in) piece of wood. Sand both square and mark the drill holes (*figure 6*). Use your 9mm (⅜in) bit to drill straight through. Clean the edges of the holes with sandpaper and glue both blocks into position. The front block is 127mm (5in) from the rear edge. The back block is 25mm (1in) from the rear edge. Put aside to set.

Fig 6   Log support block

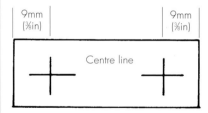

⑥ We now go back to the tractor. Along the side of the base mark a central spot, 152mm (6in) from the bumper. Support the base on an offcut and hold against a square block. Drill through with a 13mm (½in) bit, taking care when the drill breaks through. This is the rear axle hole.

⑦ Take the cab/engine assembly and apply glue over the whole base area. Press firmly onto the cab base, leaving 13mm (½in) clear behind the bumper. Align cab sides with base and leave to set.

⑧ Finally, cut four 9mm (⅜in) dowels 64mm (2½in) long. Chamfer all ends and glue into the four support block holes. A small pin hammer may be required at this stage. Once every-thing has set both halves of the toy are ready for a little extra doweling for added strength.

Fig 7   Axle block

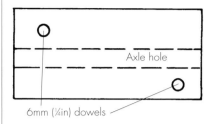

6mm (¼in) dowels

⑨ Turn both units upside down and spot-mark two 6mm (¼in) dowel holes on the axle block; one either side of the axle hole and diagonally opposite (*figure 7*). The same goes for the front axle block of the tractor. Sink a dowel through the base into the engine block and two into the cab – across the width. The last two dowels are positioned along the centre line of the bumper, about 50mm (2in) apart. Ensure all doweling is sanded flush. The two units are now ready for varnishing.

Finishing

Some people prefer working with sealers and polyurethane varnish or lacquers. For years I have worked with a water-based acrylic varnish that is both fast drying and non-toxic. Whichever you prefer, give both units a coat of sealer/varnish. When dry and the grain has risen, rub down all over with 100-grade sandpaper. Apply a second coat and dry rub down again once with a finer grade of paper. I use 150. Apply two to three more coats depending on your own requirements.

Logs for the trailer can be of various diameter doweling, sawn and chamfered to assorted lengths. They look nice finished with a non-toxic stain followed by a couple of coats of varnish. As a rule I try to ensure most of the logs fit through the windows, as most children find it fascinating to do this. It also looks effective if you use some broken branches from which various lengths can be cut.

Wheel making

I prefer to make wheels. It gives the toy a chunkier feel. The easiest way is to saw discs from 75mm x 25mm (3in x 1in) stock with hole cutters.
❶ Mark the centre line and space your discs along this. You will need four wheels of 70mm (2¾in) diameter and two at 38mm (1½in). Once the pilot drill has drilled through, allow the hole saw to cut almost through the stock.
❷ Turn the piece over, re-locate the pilot drill and allow the cutter to gently free the wheel. You will have to stop the drill to remove each wheel. Once they have all be cut, sand the faces as wells as a 3mm (⅛in) radius around both edges.
❸ Pilot drills are normally 6mm (¼in) so the four large wheels will have to be drilled out to suit the 9mm (⅜in) axle rods. As all stock varies slightly, cut three axles to a length which allows a 5mm (³⁄₁₆in) sideways movement.
❹ Chamfer the ends and glue the wheels into place, ensuring the dowel end is flush with the outer face of the wheel. ●

Other items required

● **Acrylic varnish**
David Deverill Adhesives & Coatings, Unit 13B Coppull Enterprise Centre, Mill Lane, Coppull, Chorley, Lancs PR7 5BW
Tel: 01257 793196
● **Abrasive sheets**
● **Stain** (for non-toxic paints and stains)
Westcountry Finishes Ltd, Unit 4, Station Business Park, Lwr Brimley Ind. Est, Teignmouth, Devon TQ14 8QJ
Tel: 01626 833209
● **Hole cutters**
Simbles, The Broadway, Queen's Road, Watford, Herts WD1 2LA
Tel: 01923 226052
● **Wheels**
Hobbies (Dereham) Ltd, 34-36 Swaffham Road, Dereham, Norfolk NR19 2QZ
Tel: 01362 692985

Glyn Salisbury has been making wooden toys and fretwork gifts for more than 12 years, the last 10 of which have been in full-time self-employment.
Credit for his woodworking skills must go, in the first instance, to his father's tuition. After learning all his father knew, Glyn extended his knowledge to include the art of fretwork.
Now residing in John O'Groats, he and his wife, Su, must be the most northern toymakers on the UK mainland.
He has three children, Jenny, Elizabeth and Benjamin. Also sharing the old School and Schoolhouse grounds is William (their ever faithful golden Labrador), and six ducks.

Note the subtle finish to the logs.

Take to the air, fly a boomerang

If you think about it, chucking a piece of wood into the air and having it come back to you in a few seconds is pretty incredible.
Michael Hanson *shares his secrets for successful flights*

BOOMERANG throwing develops a harmony with and an understanding of wind and air currents. A well executed throw will have the boomerang back to your hands in a few seconds.

After considerable research I found the secrets: there are no elastics or magnets and you don't need wind assistance either. It's all to do with aerodynamic lift, gyroscopic precession and good quality plywood. To achieve successful returning flights however, you only need good co-ordination and common sense.

The returning boomerang which we are concerned with here was probably peculiar to Australia and dates from at least 15,000 years ago. Aboriginals used them for sport and games in much the same way as modern boomerang throwers.

The anatomy of a traditional boomerang is shown in *figure 1*. There are two types: right handed (RH) and left handed (LH). You can see a variety of boomerangs on page 78. The plan form shape is not of paramount importance. Many different shapes can return. What is very important is the cross-section of the arms or wings. The shaping of these surfaces or airfoil is what makes it work.

To convert a picture of a RH boomerang into a LH boomerang, view the picture in a mirror placed at the side (a LH boomerang is exactly the mirror image of a RH one, as is its flight path).

Shaping

The boomerangs shown are not big. In fact modern sports boomerangs are quite small nowadays. The proven designs I've chosen all work well and fly a distance of between 25m (approx 80ft) and 30m (approx 100ft). You need the best top quality plywood you can get. Finnish birch is usually very good; 5mm ($3/16$in) or 6mm ($1/4$in) ply is ideal for the boomerangs shown. Occasionally you can get Finnish ply with really thin layers (plies). I've used 5mm ($3/16$in) wood that had 10 plies. It's easily available on the Continent, but is difficult to find in the UK. I have in the past used good thin model aircraft three ply and glued two sheets together.

If you can only get five ply (5 or 6 mm) - get the best. No sheet of ply is perfectly flat. If it has a bad warp, reject it, but if it has a slight dish - that is OK. The concave side will be the boomerang's 'top' surface. So, decide on the 'top' and find out if the thrower is right or left-handed and copy the boomerang(s) onto the ply using the squares as a guide.

The minimum tools required are: coping saw, rasp, spoke shave or Surform; one or two G-clamps, assorted sand paper and a sanding block. If you are blessed with power tools all the better. Cut out the plan form shape with your saw and then sand the edges smooth with some coarse sandpaper around a sanding block. This produces a

Michael Hanson *teaches physics at Doon Academy in Ayrshire. His interests are many, but odd aspects of flight are particularly absorbing. Boomerang miscellany takes up a lot of his time. He has more than 500 in his collection, occasionally visits boomerang competitions abroad and has organised boomerang workshops in several recent science festivals.*

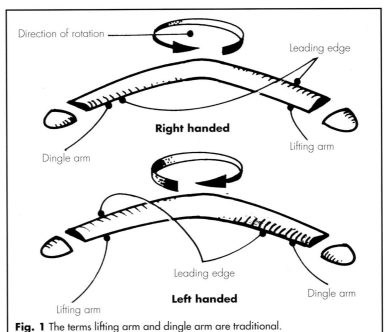

Direction of rotation

Leading edge

Right handed

Dingle arm

Lifting arm

Leading edge

Left handed

Dingle arm

Lifting arm

Fig. 1 The terms lifting arm and dingle arm are traditional.

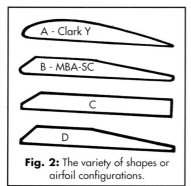

Fig. 2: The variety of shapes or airfoil configurations.

A - Clark Y
B - MBA-SC
C
D

Right: Clamp firmly and take it easy.

Below right: This is a RH boomerang shaped from 5-ply. Note the ply joins. View these constantly during the shaping process.

Bottom right: RH boomerangs ready to fly.

smooth outline as there may be a few imperfections in your sawing.

The shape of the airfoil section is the same all along each arm. I like to obtain the smooth shape commonly found on aeroplane's wings called Clark Y, but a lot of boomerang makers satisfy themselves with the MBA-SC section (Modern Boomerang Airfoil - Semi-Crude). Clark Y is in fact a smoothed and rounded version of MBA-SC (*figure 2*, A and B).

MBA-SC

1 The underside is easy - it's flat - so leave it. Refer to the plan and locate the leading edge. Fix the boomerang blank to the edge of the bench or table with the G-clamp(s) and shape the leading edges (the blunt ones) first.
2 Depending on what you've got, use a rasp, spoke shave or Surform to remove wood from the 'top' surface. I use a sanding disc in an electric drill. If you've not done this sort of thing before, practice on a piece of scrap wood first. Take a little of the wood away at a time as shown above. You can always take a bit more off but putting some back is hard. Note the plies - your contour line as shown. You end

up with *figure 2*, C.
3 Now the trailing edges - the sharp ones. Again, I recommend a little practice first. It's quite easy to take off too much. Clamp again to the edge of the bench/table, take away a little at a time and check the contours. Now you'll end up with *figure 2*, D.
4 At the elbow it is necessary to merge leading edges with trailing edges and right at the elbow the shape is symmetrical.
5 MBA-SC or Clark Y? For the former, simply round off the edges with coarse sand paper. For Clark Y you'll need to spend a bit more effort to fully round the edges. Now carefully sand all along the arms with coarse, then medium, then fine sandpaper until it's really smooth and your boomerang looks like that below. Now you've cut it, shaped it, carved it, sanded it and smoothed it, but don't finish it till you've tried it.

Decoration

Methods are many and varied. Give it another fine sand and wipe off the dust. If you like you can decorate with felt pens then seal with linseed oil or wax or you can brush/spray a couple of coats of clear varnish. The varnish gives a good foundation for further decor using:
a) Transfers or thin stickers
b) Painted stripes or spots in the Aboriginal style
c) Coloured varnish
d) Painted designs or logos
e) Stencils
f) Airbrushing
g) Pyrography

Other methods

I don't usually like to cover up the plies completely with paint. When they are still visible I think they look quite elegant. After the decor I like to give one or two more coats of clear varnish for a final glass-like finish.

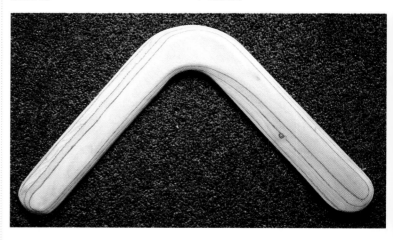

Throwing tips

1 Find a good sized field on a calm day - evenings are generally calmest. If there's a wind - go get your kite. Ideal boomerang throwing weather is perfect calm. A slight drift is acceptable however. Find its direction by dropping a few blades of grass or looking at smoke.

2 Look for short grass and no obstructions (people, cars, windows, trees) for 50m (approx 160ft) all round.

3 Grip a tip. Which one you choose doesn't matter. Choose the one which feels most comfortable. Most throwers hold the lifting arm tip, but I'm a dingle arm launcher.) But make sure that the flat surface faces away from you - i.e. the flat side is touching your palm and the 'top' faces you.

4 Turn about 45° to the right or left of the air drift.

5 Have the plane of the boomerang upright or nearly so.

6 Aim straight out and give it lots of spin. The action is much like a tennis serve.

7 Vary the angles a), b), and c), and the force and spin rates until it returns obediently. Keep practising and remember that you are the target! Go easy though as beginners get sore shoulders.

8 Always keep your eye on a flying boomerang and if it comes towards you at speed, then lay face down and cover your head.

9 When you get reliable returns and the boomerang hovers for a while before settling to *terra firma* try catching it by making a boomerang sandwich, but keep your head out of the way.

10 The best number in a boomerang throwing group is one, but if two are throwing together, have only one boomerang in the air at a time. Take it in turns.

11 Maximise common sense and keep safety in mind.

12 A good flight is a combination of a good boomerang and an intelligent throw. When you can repeat good returns throw after throw then you are getting good.

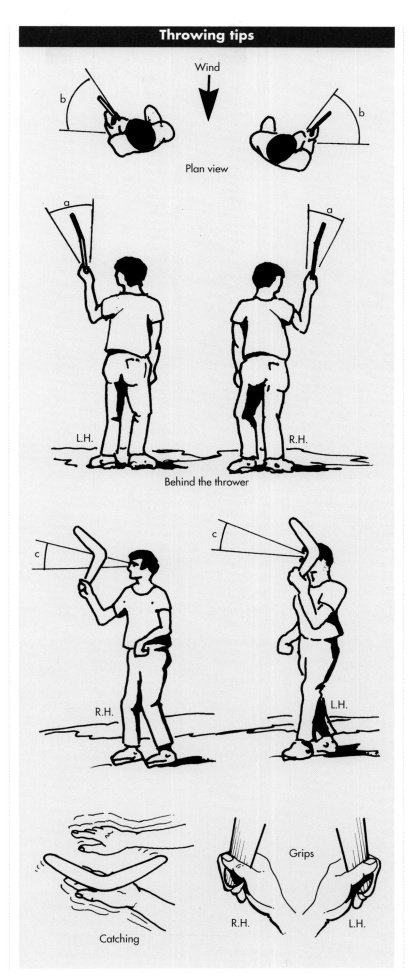

Throwing tips

Wind

Plan view

Behind the thrower

Catching

Grips

time from the centre of the circle. The shortest time for five throws and returns is the winner. The world record is 15.03 seconds and the boomerang had to go at least 20m (65ft) and each return had to be caught!

Endurance
See how many catches and/or returns you can do in five minutes. The world record for a 20m distance is 76!

Maximum time aloft
The world record for the maximum flight time between launch and landing is 2 minutes 59.94 seconds - and that was with a catch!

Consecutive catches
When you get really good try for the world record in consecutive catches. It's only 1,251!

Games and competitions
You can invent your own games, but here are a few ideas for two or more throwers similar to the competitions used in boomerang contests.
   Lay a length of string 12m (39ft) into a circle. Mark the centre spot; that's your throwing area.

Accuracy
Start your throw from the centre mark. Pick up your boomerang, don't move and have another throw. Continue until the fifth throw. Now pace out the distance of the boomerang

from the start. The shorter the distance the better.

Accuracy and catch
Throw the boomerang from within the circle. You have five throws. Twenty points is not impossible! You get:
● Point for a landing in the same field!
● Points for a catch
● Points for a landing in the circle
● Points for a catch in the circle

Fast throws
Get a stopwatch. Launch each

Alternative materials
Plywood is not the only material that can be used for boomerangs. Australian Aborigines used to select a 'natural elbow' from a curved branch or root so that the grain was always parallel to the edges. If you do this, make sure that the wood dries and cures for a few months. Other materials include aluminium sheet, fibreglass or plastic sheet (Paxolin or Perspex for example).

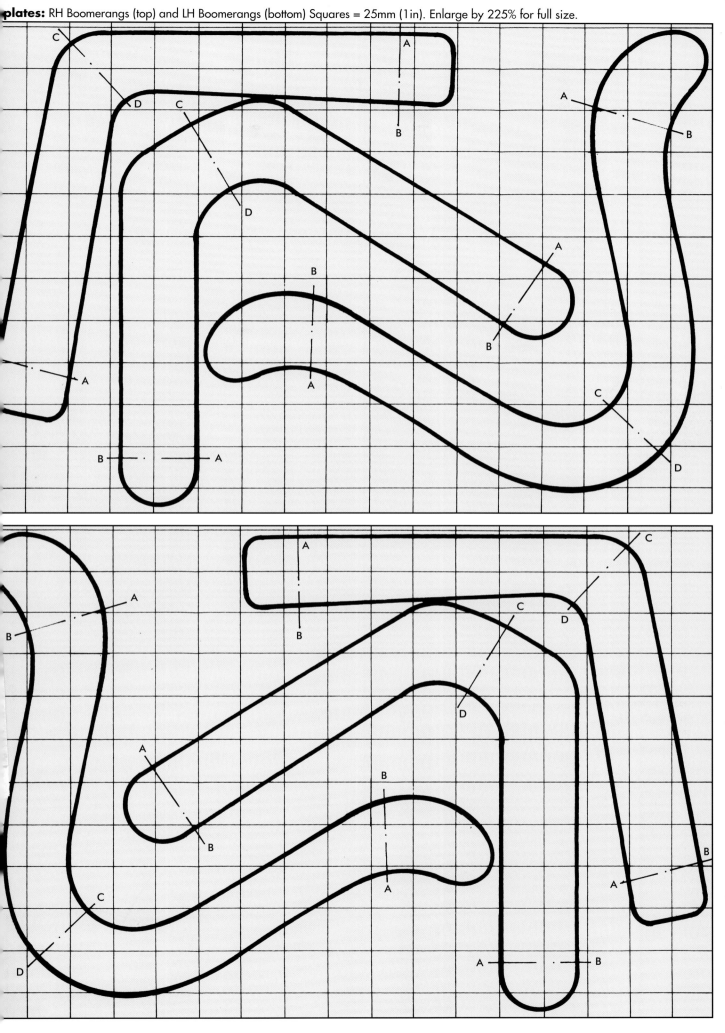

Animation for this nativity scene is provided by a simple cam system. In Part 2, on page 30, Roy explains how this brings life and movement to his creation.

Nativity ir

Materials required

- Mild steel rod, brass rod, or dowel:
  6 ($^1/_4$") dia, 610mm (24") long
  3 ($^1/_8$") dia, 610mm (24") long
- Dowel:
  3 ($^1/_4$") dia, 914mm (36") long
- PVA glue & super glue
- Pelikan Plaka Casein emulsion or acrylic paint
- Colorglaze stain:
  blue and yellow
- Medium and fine glass paper
- Panel pins 20mm ($^3/_4$") long
- Screws (No. 8 c/s) 20mm ($^3/_4$") long
- Rivets (approximately 24) plus washers

Main outside box

Refer to figures 1-4

Note: The large top displays the stable, moving and non-moving figures and animals; the smaller, bottom section houses the camrods and motor.

1 The sides comprise two bases of 6mm ($^1/_4$in) birch ply. The back panel is made of 3mm ($^1/_8$in) birch ply. Three supports holding the cams and cam axle are 20mm ($^3/_4$in) pine or ply.

2 The bottom pine supports are secured with 20mm ($^3/_4$in) counter-sunk screws to hold the bottom and middle bases together. Before screwing the bases together, drill a hold just over 6mm ($^1/_4$in) dia to hold the cam axle in the first two supports.

3 Two pieces of brass tube slightly bigger than the diameter of the cam axle are pushed into the support panels to hold the cam axle.

Cutting list

Type of wood	Size	
Plywood	6mm x 1,220mm x 1,220mm	($^1/_4$" x 48" x 48")
	3mm x 1,220mm x 1,220mm	($^1/_8$" x 48" x 48")
Microply	18mm x 18mm x 657mm	($^3/_4$" x $^3/_4$" x $^7/_8$")
Pine	20mm x 100mm x 914mm	($^3/_4$" x 4" x 36")

motion

Roy Anderson brings new meaning to the story of Christ's nativity with this fully animated toy

Roy Anderson *was originally a signwriter with combined skills in poster writing and silk-screen printing. The great storm of 1987 in Britain provided more wood than usual and his interest in woodcarving took root. Roy's wife and son also became interested in automata which has proved to be "fascinating and educational".*

Part 1: Construction

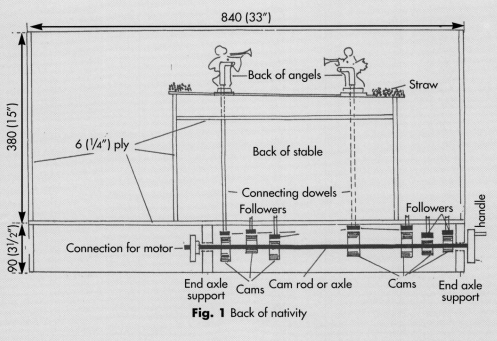

Fig. 1 Back of nativity

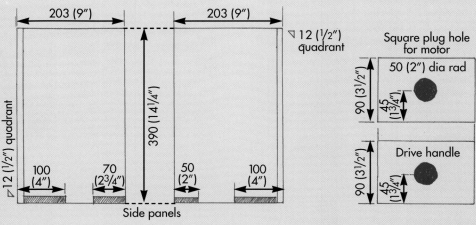

Side panels

Square plug hole for motor

Fig. 2

Bottom base with cams

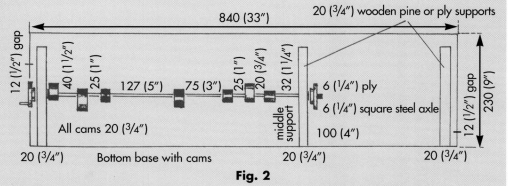

Fig. 3 Middle base with position of figures & animals

Note: The last support on the base (right side) does not need a hole as the cam axle does not extend full length.

4 Screw both sides panels to the second base (*figure 2*) with quadrants at the back to support the back panel.

5 Screw the back panel (*figure 4*) onto the side panels and supports. This back panel is slightly higher at the bottom with an insert for the motor (*figures 1 & 4*).

Note: do not glue any panels as they have to be dismantled for decoration.

Stable

Refer to figures 5-9

1 Use 6mm (1/4in) birch ply for the sides and lower curved roof; 3mm (1/8in) ply for the top roof and 12mm (1/2in) ply or pine to attach microply for the stable curve.

2 Fix together 12mm (1/2in) ply or pine and 6mm (1/4in) ply with some masking tape and then cut out the curve.

3 Screw side panels to the curved base. Notice that both slants on the sides are slightly different as the roof slopes on the side as well as the front.

4 Fix lower curved roof with panel pins. Do not nail them right in as they have to be removed.

5 Attach the top roof, cut to shape, before fixing *figure 8* to the top side panels with panel pins (not too deep for removal).

6 The back is covered with 6mm (1/4in) ply fixed between the lower and top roof.

Fixing microply for stable curve

1 Use a cardboard template. Hold the card against the bottom 12mm (1/2in) pine base curve and lower roof curve.

2 The top of the curve can be finished to the lower roof as the top roof will hide the opening.

3 Pin the microply panel to the lower roof and base curve.

Fixing straw roof

1 Cut out hessian or canvas to suit the size of the roof.

2 Tie a length of straw in

bundles to match the width of the roof and attach to hessian with thread, avoiding squares. These can be glued to the roof with PVA, but not until the squares have been fixed for the angels and the holes drilled to hold the 'follower' steel rod connector.

Figures

Refer to figures A-G

Note: all figures are cut out by fretsaw. Heads, hats, arms and legs can be glued onto each figure for additional depth and detail.

1 All are cut from 3mm (¹/₈in) ply. It is best if all items are painted before cutting out.

2 Sheets of ply are cut to small pieces approx 305mm x 305mm (12in x 12in) and given a coat of matt or satin clear varnish.

3 When dry the drawings are traced onto the board. Drawings can be painted with Plaka paint, acrylic or gouache.

4 When dry (about 15min), a coat of matt or satin clear varnish can be applied. When dry (overnight), the figures can be cut out.

5 Rivet holes are drilled for moving parts (before parts are cut out).

6 Bare ply on the outside edge can be given a coat of black.

Rivets

1 These are made of metal, 3mm (¹/₈in) dia, 10mm (³/₈in) long. Holes drilled in ply are slightly bigger than 3mm (¹/₈in) as there has to have plenty of movement. When joining the body and arms, the holes are aligned and the rivet inserted.

2 Place a small washer inside the bottom of the rivet. Strike a metal punch on the bottom of the rivet until the end forms a mushroom, making a secure joint.

Note: In Part 2, on page 30, Roy explains how to bring life and movement to the nativity scene.

Suppliers

W Hobby, Knights Hill Square, London, SE27 OHH. Telephone: 0181-761-4244

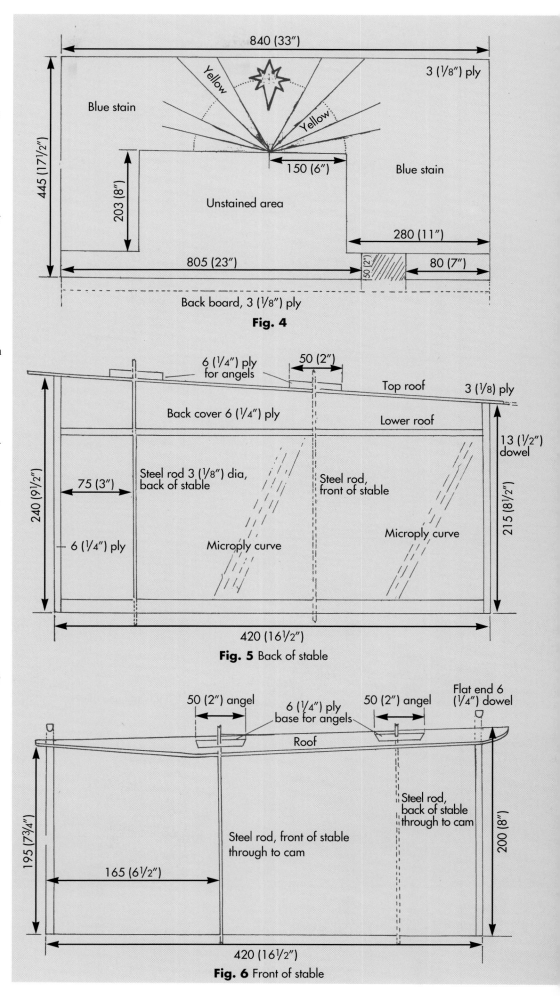

Fig. 4

Fig. 5 Back of stable

Fig. 6 Front of stable

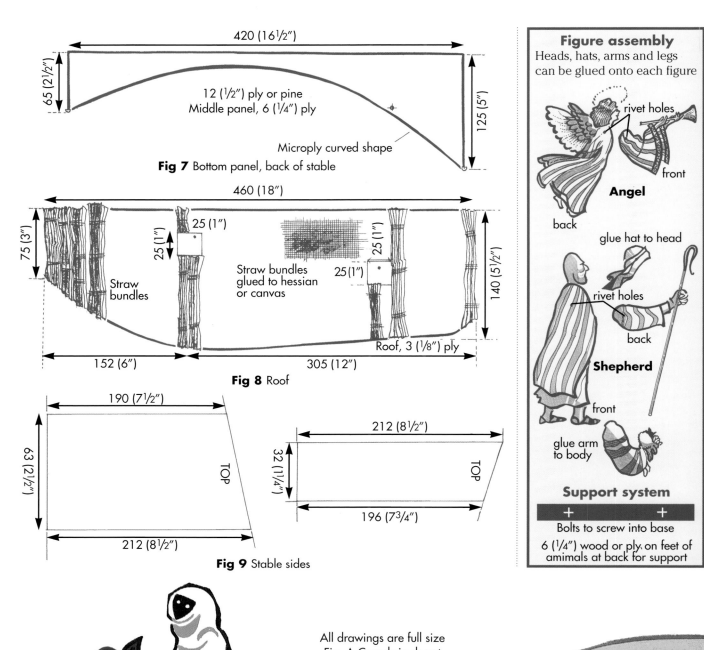

420 (16½")

65 (2½")

125 (5")

12 (½") ply or pine
Middle panel, 6 (¼") ply

Microply curved shape

Fig 7 Bottom panel, back of stable

460 (18")

75 (3")

25 (1")
25 (1")

Straw
bundles

Straw bundles
glued to hessian
or canvas

25 (1")
25 (1")
140 (5½")

152 (6")

305 (12")

Roof, 3 (⅛") ply

Fig 8 Roof

190 (7½")

63 (2½")

TOP

212 (8½")

212 (8½")

32 (1¼")

196 (7¾")

TOP

Fig 9 Stable sides

Figure assembly
Heads, hats, arms and legs
can be glued onto each figure

rivet holes

front

Angel

back

glue hat to head

rivet holes

back

Shepherd

front

glue arm
to body

Support system
+   +

Bolts to screw into base

6 (¼") wood or ply on feet of
animals at back for support

All drawings are full size
Fig. A Camels in desert

Fig. B Date tree

Fig. C Shepherd

Fig. D Lamb

Fig. E Donkey

Fig. F Hen and Mouse

Fig.G Sitting Donkey

For details of construction, including materials required, see Part 1, on pages 24 - 29.

Nativity in

Moving figures
Refer to figures for examples
1 Large shepherd
A rivet is fixed at back of figure. A large countersunk hole is drilled in front arm before gluing on front of body; a follower strut is curved to the arm. Figure attached to base.
2 Small shepherd
Strut curved to arm, rivet at front. Figure attached to base.
3 Shepherd boy
Strut curved to arm, rivet at front. Figure attached to base.
4 Joseph and angel

Joseph is connected to first angel (front side of stable) with steel rod 3mm (1/8in) and one cam fixed on based, with Mary and Jesus at back; 3mm (1/8in) dowel glued on as rook.
5 1st wise man
Rivet outside in middle of body, single base fitting.
6 2nd wise man
Same as above.
7 3rd wise man and angel
Same as above. Follower connected to second angel with steel rod 3mm (1/8in) dia back side of stable.

Motionless figures and animals
Paint in similar fashion to moving figures; fix to base with wood support 6mm (1/4in) sq with bolts and nuts.

Motor
Refer to figure 1
I used a spit roaster 230/250V motor, to run on domestic electricity. It runs slowly and is connected to the model via a square rod. The motor is inserted in the end driving wheel of the model when

30   WOODEN TOY PROJECTS

Roy Anderson *was originally a signwriter with combined skills in poster writing and silk-screen printing. The great storm of 1987 in Britain provided more wood than usual and his interest in woodcarving took root. Roy's wife and son also became interested in automata which has proved to be "fascinating and educational".*

motion

Roy Anderson *now brings life and movement to his nativity model*

required for display and operated with a switch on the outside of the model.

Alternatively, you can use a BBQ battery motor. As it is shaped like a torch at the back, a curved wooden bracket plus a front support near the driving wheel should be suitable for fixing. The square driving connection is the same size as the spit roaster motor.

Cams and followers

1 Cams can be cut from thicker wood (pine or any offcut)

about 20mm (³/₄in) to an egg shape with a hole drilled slightly off centre. This is a tight fit on the cam axle which is made of steel, brass rod or doweling 6mm (¹/₄in) dia.

2 Followers can be from of 20mm (³/₄in) wood. A long follower is used for Joseph and the angel, and the third wise man and angel as they are both used on a single cam.

One angel follower is placed behind Joseph, the other angel follower is placed behind the third wise man.

3 Experiment with the cam and followers to raise and lower the arm and body. Sometimes a slice can be taken off cams, sometimes a slice added until the correct shape is found (masking tape is ideal for this).

4 When the arm or body is moved it should fall back on its own weight. If it doesn't, small pieces of wood glued to the back should do the trick. When each figure moves correctly, cams can be fixed to the cam axle with a c/s screw.

5 Thread the cams onto the axle rod from left to right, with the middle support unscrewed until all cams are fixed.

6 Re-screw middle support and fix on driving wheel for motor.
Note: all parts, figures, animals stable, etc, are fixed with a handle at one end for a trial run. If this is successful, parts can be secured tightly.

Decoration

1 The back board and side panels are decorated with Rustin's Colorglaze. Yellow is applied first with masking tape either side of the rays and star. Three coats are suitable, sanding down between applications.

2 Apply blue stain on the side panels and the rest of the back board. A section is left blank in the middle as it will be covered by the stable. The stable will not be decorated.

Suppliers

W Hobby, Knights Hill Square, London, SE27 0HH. Tel: 0181-761-4244

Crook sanded at end and put into dowel rod

Dowel rod glued on as crook

Small shepherd

Arm glued onto frame, 3 (¹/₈")

Rivet in back

140 (5¹/₂")

Back view

Large shepherd

Side view

Rivets

6 (¹/₄") wood moving lever

3 (¹/₈") dowel

Follower

Cam

Dowel inserted into follower

6 (¹/₄") cam rod or axle

Back view

20 (³/₄") No8 c/s bolt & nut

6 (¹/₄") follower

6 (¹/₄") follower

45 (1³/₄")

6 (¹/₄") support

Boy shepherd

6 (¹/₄") follower

25 (1") No8 c/s screw Small shepherd

38 (1¹/₂")

6 (¹/₄") support

6 (¹/₄") ply base for moving shepherds

Large shepherd

178 (7")

Side vi

Shepherd boy

Angel

Back view

To follower
with Joseph

Side view

Fastener for
holding dowel

Rivet

To support angel

Block on roof
of stables

To Joseph

Back view

Side view

100 (4")

Joseph

Large axle hole

Top body
of Joseph

100 (4")

Bottom body
of Joseph

To angel

Side view

Back view

Back view

**6 (¹/₄") support
to hold wise man**

●Hole for follower

Side view

2nd wise man

1st wise man

Top body

127 (5") –
Rivet

Bottom body

Back view

Side view

●Hole for follower

⊖ 8 (³/₄") bolt

45 (1³/₄")

82 (3¹/₄")

Mary & Baby Jesus

100 (4")

6 (¹/₄") support, glue on base

82 (3¹/₄")

6 (¹/₄") hole for follower

33 (1/8") gap to hold Mary & Jesus

Groove to hold foot

178 (7")

Joseph

Gap to hold foot

20 (3/4")

Support for Mary, Baby Jesus & Joseph

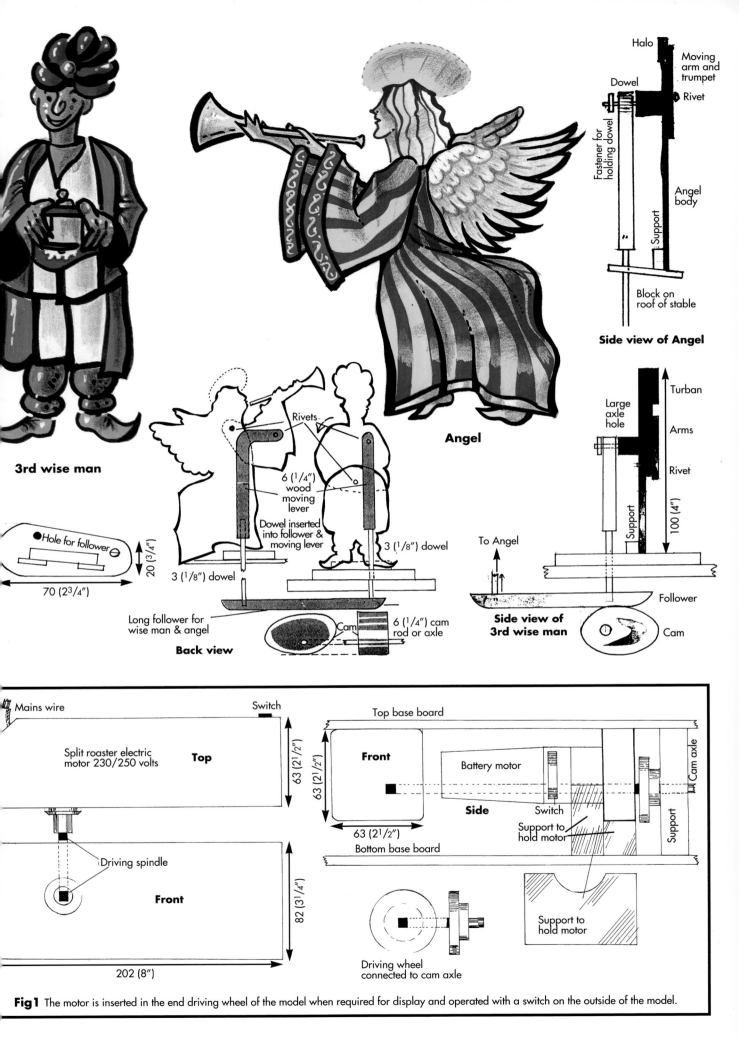

3rd wise man

Hole for follower

20 (³/4")

70 (2³/4")

Halo

Moving arm and trumpet

Dowel

Rivet

Fastener for holding dowel

Angel body

Support

Block on roof of stable

Side view of Angel

Rivets

6 (¹/4") wood moving lever

Dowel inserted into follower & moving lever

3 (¹/8") dowel

3 (¹/8") dowel

Angel

Long follower for wise man & angel

Cam

6 (¹/4") cam rod or axle

Back view

Turban

Large axle hole

Arms

Rivet

100 (4")

Support

To Angel

Follower

Side view of 3rd wise man

Cam

Mains wire

Switch

Top base board

Split roaster electric motor 230/250 volts

Top

63 (2¹/2")

Front

Battery motor

Cam axle

63 (2¹/2")

Side

Switch

Support

63 (2¹/2")

Support to hold motor

Driving spindle

Front

82 (3¹/4")

Bottom base board

Support to hold motor

202 (8")

Driving wheel connected to cam axle

Fig 1 The motor is inserted in the end driving wheel of the model when required for display and operated with a switch on the outside of the model.

Old **London** Bridge

Terry Lawrence re-creates a famous landmark that brings a taste of history to your fingertips

This is not the bridge which has been re-erected at Lake Havasu in Arizona, but its predecessor. It was started in 1176 AD, completed in 1209 and it needed constant repair during its 622-years of life.

It had 19 arches all of different sizes. The piers were built on flat piles called starlings, each wider than its pier, and so causing the water under each arch to flow fiercely, with consequent erosion.

The bridge was covered in houses and shops, many corbelled, ie, projecting over the side of the bridge. This may have been convenient for toilet purposes, but was not really safe, as on at least one occasion, a row of houses fell off into the River Thames.

The model has been simplified and I have made only six spans over seven piers. I have standardised the length of each span though there is provision for wider spans if you wish. The whole thing is really an up-market set of bricks (all components are made of oak) with endless arrangements possible. You may prefer not to paint the pieces though smooth sanded wood can look quite attractive.

If you do paint your model I will describe a simple method of painting the windows which otherwise could get a little tedious if done with a fine brush.

I have not provided a cutting list as you will probably wish to vary the number of spans of your model and the number of houses.
However, you will need:
- Timber 75mm x 6mm (3in x ¼in) for the roadways of the standard spans
- 113mm x 6mm (4½in x ¼in) for the wide spans
- All arches are cut from 44mm x 6mm (1¾in x ¼in)
- The piers are cut from 32mm x 50mm (1¼in x 2in) timber

All cutting can be done on the smallest scroll saw, but you may find a bandsaw useful for thicker pieces.

Old London Bridge comes to life. Here we see the southern end of the bridge.

Construction

Pier

A standard pier comprises a piece of wood 50mm (2in) high, 32mm (1¼in) wide and 140mm (5½in) long. It has a cut-out in the top surface, 75mm (3in) long and 6mm (¼in) deep to accept a section of roadway. Each end is pointed and the piece is glued to a flat starling 44mm (1¾in) wide and 191mm (7½in) long, cut from 6mm (¼in) thick timber. As you see, the 6mm (¼in) projection of the starling at each side of the pier is a shelf to accept the base of each arch.

❶ Mark the 32mm x 50mm (1¼in x 2in) timber at 25mm (1in) from each end and mark the top face along its centre. Draw the two lines to mark the V-point at each end and cut out on the scroll saw with a coarse blade (or on the bandsaw). Sand the surfaces. These angled cuts leave 6mm (¼in) of pier at full width before the cut-out for the roadway.

❷ Cut a starling from a flat plate from 44mm x 6mm (1¾in x ¼in) timber as shown in the drawing, and

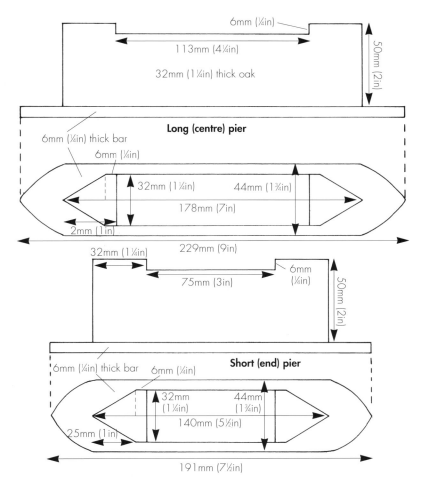

6mm (¼in)
113mm (4½in)
32mm (1¼in) thick oak
50mm (2in)

Long (centre) pier

6mm (¼in) thick bar
6mm (¼in)
32mm (1¼in) 44mm (1¾in)
178mm (7in)
2mm (1in)
229mm (9in)

32mm (1¼in)
75mm (3in)
6mm (¼in)
50mm (2in)

Short (end) pier

6mm (¼in) thick bar 6mm (¼in)
32mm (1¼in) 44mm (1¾in)
140mm (5½in)
25mm (1in)
191mm (7½in)

round the ends. Glue the pier to the starling which is 25mm (1in) longer at each end than the pier and 6mm (¼in) wider on each side. Repeat for as many piers as you want.

❸ I have made some centre spans at 113mm (4½in) wide, which are useful for central shops. These require longer piers and starlings. As the drawings show just add 38mm (1½in) to the length of each including the top cut-out.

❹ If you decide on a single wide span, you will need two long piers to accommodate it. If you have two wide spans, you will need three long piers.

Arch

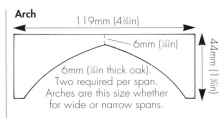

119mm (4¾in)
6mm (¼in)
44mm (1¾in)

6mm (¼in thick oak).
Two required per span.
Arches are this size whether
for wide or narrow spans.

Arch

❶ An arch piece is 119mm (4¾in) wide and cut from timber 44mm x 6mm (1¾in x ¼in). This size is correct, whatever the width of each span. Cut two arches for each span.

The centre spans are cut from 6mm (¼in) thick oak.

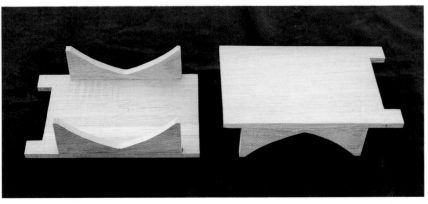

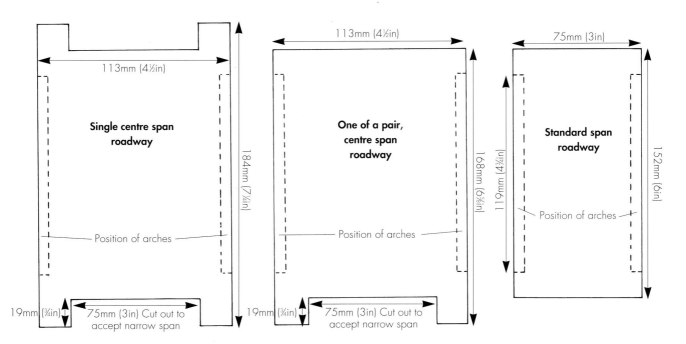

Single centre span roadway

113mm (4½in)

184mm (7¼in)

Position of arches

19mm (¾in)

75mm (3in) Cut out to accept narrow span

One of a pair, centre span roadway

113mm (4½in)

168mm (6⅝in)

119mm (4¾in)

Position of arches

19mm (¾in)

75mm (3in) Cut out to accept narrow span

Standard span roadway

75mm (3in)

152mm (6in)

Position of arches

Roadway

1 A standard span has a horizontal roadway piece of 152mm x 75mm (6in x 3in). Cut from 6mm (¼in) thick timber. Cut as many as you need. If you copy my model you will need four as the centre two spans are wide ones.

Wide span

1 In order to avoid unsightly gaps I have made the 113mm (4½in) wide pieces so that they accommodate the ends of the standard 75mm (3in) wide sections.

2 If you have just a single wide span cut the roadway piece from 113mm (4½in) wide timber to a length of 184mm (7¼in). Make a cut-out centrally at each end 75mm x 19mm (3in x ¾in) deep. Note that the very ends of this piece will cover the piers, ie flush with the outer faces, leaving the cut-out to accept the adjacent standard roadway pieces; the ends of which will reach the centre line of the pier,

3 If you have two wide spans, then cut the roadway pieces from 113mm (4½in) wide timber to 168mm (6⅝in) lengths, each with a cut-out at one end only. The plain end of each of these pieces will then meet at the centre line of the centre pier, and the other recessed ends will accept the standard widths of adjacent roadway.

....

Right **The standard bridge has two 113mm (4½in) centre spans. Note the optional single span.**

Arches

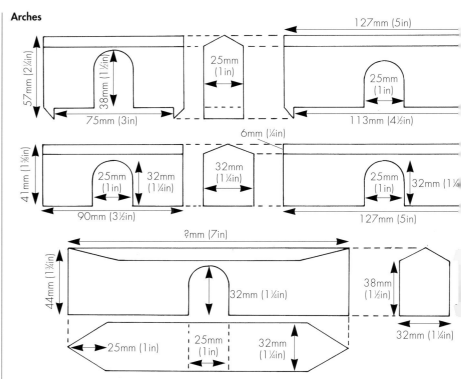

127mm (5in)

57mm (2¼in)

38mm (1½in)

75mm (3in)

25mm (1in)

25mm (1in)

113mm (4½in)

41mm (1⅝in)

25mm (1in)

32mm (1¼in)

90mm (3½in)

6mm (¼in)

32mm (1¼in)

25mm (1in)

32mm (1¼

127mm (5in)

?mm (7in)

44mm (1¾in)

32mm (1¼in)

25mm (1in)

25mm (1in)

32mm (1¼in)

38mm (1½in)

32mm (1¼in)

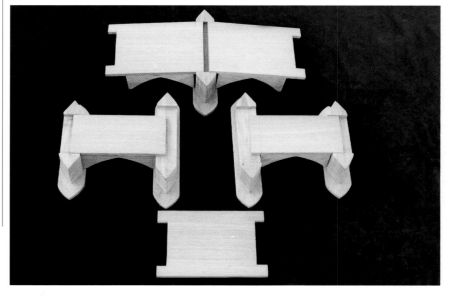

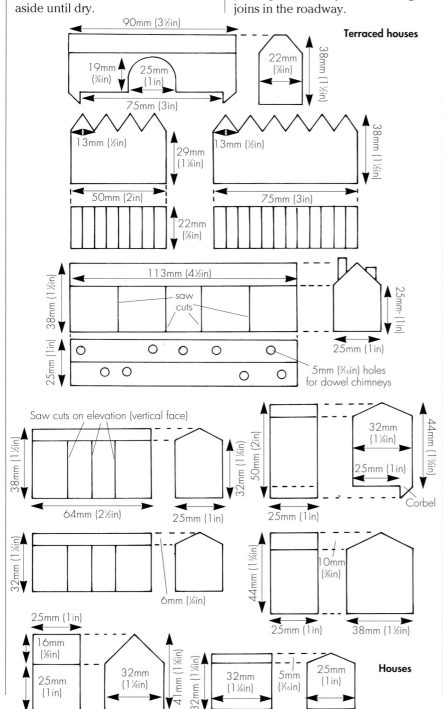

Left **The oak piers; the end piers accept 75mm (3in) wide roadways while the centre piers accept 113mm (4½in) wide roadways.**

❹ Just be aware that in the case of double (or multiple) wide spans, the arch will be glued 16mm (⅝in) in from the plain end of the wide roadway piece.

❺ You should now glue the arches to the roadway pieces at 90º, and set aside until dry.

Houses

I have provided drawings for six buildings of different width, each with a central arch to allow pedestrians and small carts to pass through. These pieces fit across the bridge; three are corbelled, ie bevelled at 45º at the lower outer corners. The flat-bottomed pieces at 32mm (1¼in) wide are useful for placing above the piers, covering the joins in the roadway.

I have drawn several blocks of terraced houses, some with sawtooth roofing, some with mansard, and some with a simple pitch. All are easily cut from scrap or you can chamfer strips of wood of the correct cross-section on the bench saw or bandsaw, and then cross-cut single dwellings or blocks of houses.

❶ Bear in mind that the space between piers is 113mm (4½in) and you can cut widths which will fit or create multiples which will fit within this length.

❷ If you decide to paint a block of terraced houses using different colours it is useful to define the dividing lines between each house, so the paint line shall be vertical; you don't have to wait for one colour to dry before painting the adjacent house. Just push the block against the moving scroll saw blade and cut to a depth of say .8mm (¹∕₃₂in) only.

Terraced houses

Houses

Looking south: rondavels on the wide centre spans are shops. Note that the long arches hide joins in the roadway.

❸ You can add chimneys if you wish: 6mm (¼in) or 5mm (³∕₁₆in) dowel of assorted lengths. Drill the holes in the roofs first, then paint. Drop a spot of glue into the hole, stain the piece of dowel with wood dye, roll it on blotting paper or

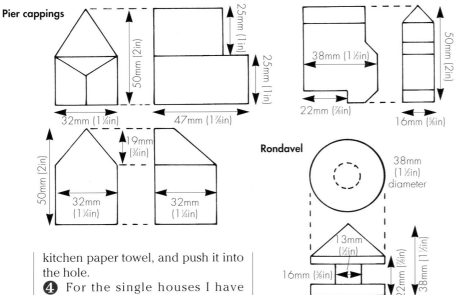

Pier cappings

25mm (1in)
25mm (1in)
50mm (2in)
32mm (1¼in)
47mm (1⅞in)

38mm (1½in)
22mm (⅞in)
50mm (2in)
16mm (⅝in)

19mm (¾in)
50mm (2in)
32mm (1¼in)
32mm (1¼in)

Rondavel

38mm (1½in) diameter

13mm (½in)
16mm (⅝in)
22mm (⅞in)
38mm (1½in)
38mm (1½in)
38mm (1½in)

kitchen paper towel, and push it into the hole.

❹ For the single houses I have drawn six examples though you can use your own designs. Those which are not corbelled are most easily cut off a length of wood ripped to the correct cross-section as before.

❺ The two little rondavels were turned from scrap on the lathe, held in a compression chuck. They fit easily between the rows of houses on the wide spans of the bridge.

Black Jacobean oak stain was used to finish the piers and arches, followed by painting the stones with matt enamel.

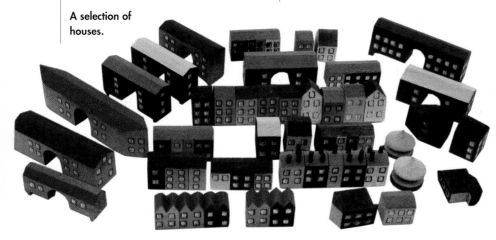

Painting

I have used colours which are close to those used in the 13th century.

A selection of houses.

You may think them rather dull. Well, they are and if your child wants bright colours, then why not?

❶ Matt colours look better than gloss and I used Humbrol matt enamels. For the bridge structure itself, ie, piers and archways, I used a wood dye, in black Jacobean oak shade. This dried overnight to give a dark hue which still allowed the wood grain to show through.

❷ The stones around the arches were painted freehand with tan matt enamel. Put a roughly triangular patch at the apex of the arch as a keystone, then paint random stones below on either curve.

❸ For the piers, I painted (with the same enamel) horizontal and vertical lines to simulate courses of masonry. I did this on the pier only, not the starling, and not where it would be hidden by the arch when assembled. It took about five minutes per pier.

❹ I was daunted by the number of windows on the houses, as it is difficult to paint very small oblongs and achieve neatness and corner squareness. The solution was to print them and I made two small rubber stamps. Cut two pieces from a pencil eraser (I used a white plastic eraser), 6mm (¼in) to 10mm (⅜in) square, and about 50mm (2in long). With a scalpel or other sharp blade, cut the end of one piece of rubber to an oblong 5mm x 6mm (³⁄₁₆in x ¼in). Cut one end of the other piece of rubber to an oblong 10mm x 6mm (⅜in x ¼in) then with the point of the blade at an inward-pointing angle, remove the centre of the oblong to leave a frame, each side of which is 1.5mm (¹⁄₁₆in) wide. The first piece will print your windows, the second piece the frames. Spread a little matt enamel on a piece of coated cardboard, tap the printing block into the film of paint and apply it to one of the houses. Dip in paint for every application and do the windows first. This way any slight error in verticality can be compensated by printing the frame over the window. ●

Terry Lawrence began making toys for his two sets of twins more than 30 years ago when, as a low-paid civil servant, he was unable to afford shop-bought playthings.

He soon found that what he made was better than the commercially-produced variety, and his children had more fun with them. In addition, there was great satisfaction in making individual designs for his own family.

Terry's toy ideas now appear regularly in magazines. His book *Turning Wooden Toys*, published by GMC Publications Ltd, includes projects ranging from a simple set of colourmix tops to his version of Jules Verne's submarine 'Nautilus', with oval-turned hull.

This jolly clown puppet by Jeff and Jennie Loader will delight all the family. He is easy for little hands to operate – see him walk, sit, jump, wave and dance!

puppet
on a string

Suitable for beginners to make, the project requires only basic tools and knowledge.

Construction

Hands and boots

1 Transfer the hand profile twice onto 6mm birch plywood and the boot profile, again twice, onto 12mm birch plywood. Cut them using a fretsaw.

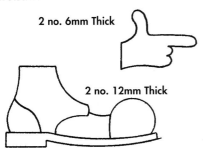

2 no. 6mm Thick

2 no. 12mm Thick

Hand & Boot Patterns Scale – full size

Wooden parts – Materials

3 x 12mm wood balls
2 x 18mm wood balls
1 x 40mm wood balls
Lengths of 6mm diameter hardwood dowel – 1 x 26mm; 2 x 24mm; 2 x 15mm
Length of 3mm diameter hardwood dowel – 1 x 10mm
Hardwood scraps –
    1 x 65mm x 30mm x 20mm
    2 x 120mm lengths of 12mm x 12mm
6mm Birch plywood –
    small scraps for hands
12mm Birch plywood –
    small scraps for boots
1625 mm (64in) approx length of fine string, such as that used on luggage labels, would be ideal, but is hard to find these days. A good alternative, which we used, is Cotes Mercer Crochet 10 White thread.

2 Centrally, into the wrist of each hand, drill a 3mm diameter hole to a depth of 4mm.

TIP: A simple method of determining the correct depth measurement of a hole whilst drilling, is to wrap a piece of adhesive tape around the drill bit. Ensure the depth required will be the distance from the tip of the drill's spurs (if using a wood bit) to the leading edge of the adhesive tape. Cease drilling when the leading edge of the tape reaches the surface of the workpiece.

3 Into each 12mm diameter wood ball drill a 3mm diameter hole to a depth of 5mm. When drilling, hold each wood ball in a vice and, if possible, use a hand drill.

4 Cut two 15mm lengths from a sanded length of 3mm diameter hardwood dowel rod. Glue a hardwood ball to one end, and a

1 Hand drilling dowel hole in the hand using tape to gauge the correct depth measurement
2 Hand drilling dowel hole in the boot using a depth gauge

hand to the other end of each length of dowel.

5 Drill a 6mm diameter hole to a depth of 8mm centrally into the top of each boot.

6 Into each 18mm diameter wood ball drill a 6mm diameter hole to a depth of 8mm.

7 Cut two 24mm lengths from a sanded length of 6mm diameter hardwood dowel rod. Glue a hardwood ball and boot to each end of each dowel.

Head and Torso

1 Cut and prepare the rectangular block that will be the torso of the clown. Drill the neck socket hole. This is 10mm deep and 6mm in diameter.

2 A 40mm diameter hardwood ball is used for the clown's head. Into this drill a 10mm deep, 6mm diameter neck socket hole and a 5mm deep, 3mm diameter nose connecting hole.

3 Cut a 26mm long length from a sanded length of 6mm hardwood dowel. Glue this dowel into the head's neck socket. Then glue the 'neck' into the torso.

4 The nose is a 12mm diameter hardwood ball. Hold it in a vice and, with a hand drill, drill a 3mm diameter hole to a depth of 5mm. Attach the nose to the head with a glued 10mm length 3mm diameter hardwood dowel. *(If you do not have a vice and are using a hand drill, get a friend to hold the ball in place with some pliers. – Ed)*

All wooden components complete prior to painting

Homemade painting jig

5 Paint the head, hands and boots using enamel modelling paints.

TIP: A simple drying jig can be made from scrap wood in order to accommodate the freshly painted components (see photo). The makeshift jig shown had been used for many different projects and has proved invaluable. The clown's hands and boots are attached to the jig by custom made wire hooks hung from panel pins.

Controlling cross

1 Prepare a length of 12mm x 12mm hardwood. Cut two 120mm lengths. These two lengths are joined by means of a cross halving joint.

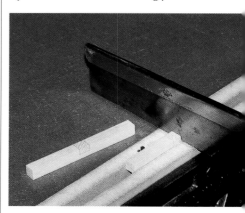

Cutting down the waste side of each line to make the joint on the controlling cross

2 At the centre of each length, mark the thickness of its mate. With a combination of try square and marking knife, mark two lines across the surface and down the sides of each length. Set a marking gauge to half the thickness of the lengths and mark along the side of each length to

Head & Torso

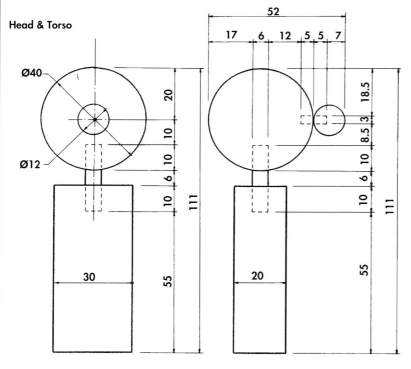

Chiselling away the waste

indicate the depth of the material to be removed. Using a gent's saw, or fine-toothed dovetail saw, cut down the waste side of each line (see photo). Then carefully chisel the waste from each length.

3 Each length should now be as illustrated below (Controlling cross component), and fit snugly together to form a cross.

4 The string holes can now be drilled. Note that one hole (which will be used to retain the string that controls the puppet hands and arms) is horizontal to the other three (see lower drawing).

5 Assemble the cross using a suitable wood glue and clamp together until the glue has set.

6 Finish the controlling cross as you wish. A couple of coats of teak oil was used in the example.

Fabric costume – Materials

Scraps of material
Matching sewing thread

General instructions

1 Transfer the patterns onto light-weight paper (tissue paper is fine), marking all details given. 6mm seams are allowed throughout. Join the fabric right sides facing, edges level and with any marks aligned.

2 Cut all pieces as directed.

Controlling cross component

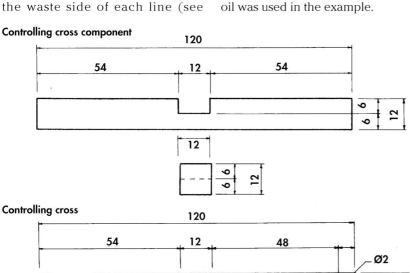

Controlling cross

All pattern pieces cut out, and centre costume seam sewn

Hat

1 Press under the seam allowance of the hat brim. Pin in place and sew. Sew up the seam, making a cone shape. Tie off the threads at the top of the hat. Trim away excess seam allowance. Turn the hat right side out and press.

Sewing the hat brim

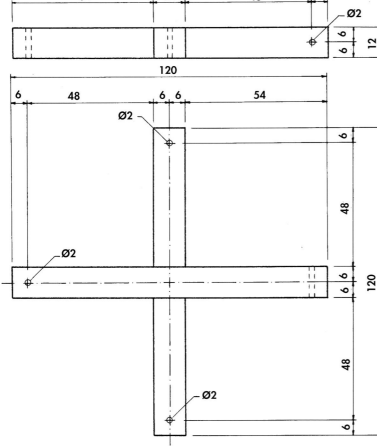

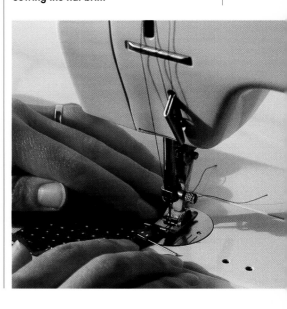

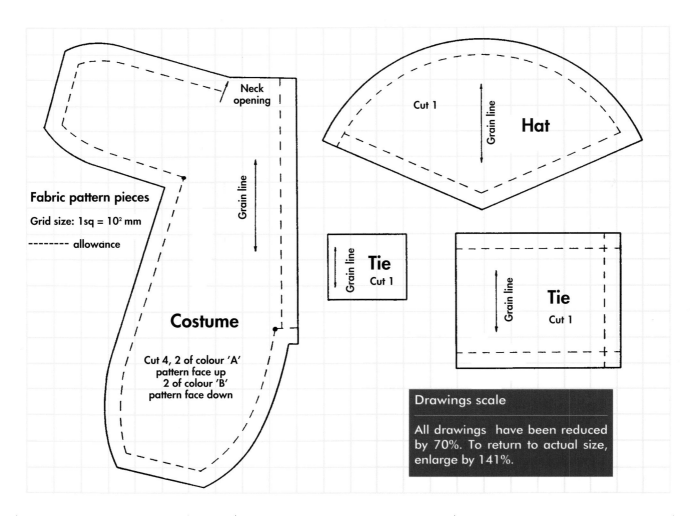

Fabric pattern pieces

Grid size: 1sq = 10² mm

-------- allowance

Neck opening

Grain line

Costume

Cut 4, 2 of colour 'A'
pattern face up
2 of colour 'B'
pattern face down

Cut 1

Grain line

Hat

Grain line

Tie
Cut 1

Grain line

Tie
Cut 1

Drawings scale

All drawings have been reduced by 70%. To return to actual size, enlarge by 141%.

Costume

❶ Place the two front costume pieces right sides together, pin and sew along centre seam. Repeat for back costume pieces. Press the seams to one side.

❷ Press under all the seam allowances at the cuffs and trouser bottoms. Sew in place.

❸ With right sides together, pin and sew shoulder seams to balance marks. Press shoulder seams open.

Stitching around the neck opening

Press neck seam allowance under. Stitch around the resulting neck slot in a box formation (see photo).

❹ Pin the inside leg seams together, matching centre seam. Sew from ankle to ankle through balance marks at gusset. Snip to balance marks at gusset.

❺ Pin underarm and side seams matching balance marks. Sew from ankle to wrist on each side. Snip at underarm.

❻ Turn right side out through the neck. Press.

Bow tie

❶ **Large piece**. Fold right sides together and stitch down the long and one short side. Snip away excess seam allowance at corners. Turn right side out. Fold in the seam allowance on the remaining side and sew together by hand.

❷ **Small piece**. Fold the two seam allowances, one over the other to the back, making a long, thin rectangle. Press.

❸ Gather the large tie piece to make a bow shape. Wrap the small tie piece around the centre and stitch it into place at the back.

❹ Sew the back of the bow tie onto the neck of the clown's costume.

Final assembly

Materials

Length of fine string or thread.

Cuff and ankle gathering

Starting at the underarm seam, sew immediately below the cuff, stitching by hand using a running stitch. Leave a long end at the start and end of this stitching. This will act as the gathering thread. Repeat for the other cuff and both trouser bottoms.

Body

Insert the wooden body of the clown through the neck of his costume (photo 10). It is a tight fit, so do this with care! When fully in place, sew up each side of the neck of his costume to prevent the body pulling out.

Stringing

❶ Drill out a small pilot hole in the centre top of the head to accommodate a small brass roundhead screw. (The size of screw will depend on the thickness of string used. We used No 2 12mm (½in) screws. If thicker string is used, a broader screw would also have to be used, because the head size holds the string in place

Below **Inserting the body of the clown through the neck of his costume**
Bottom **Attaching the head controlling string**

together with the glue.) Insert the screw, leaving enough space to wrap the string around it.
❷ Position the hat on the head and find the point immediately above the screw. (See photo). Remove hat and thread the head controlling string through the hat at the appropriate point. Wrap the string around the screw and tighten the screw down firmly.
❸ Stick the hat down using glue around the brim.
❹ Tie a length of string around each ankle. Secure each knot to the front of the ankle using instant glue. Trim away the loose ends.
❺ Tie one end of a length of string to one wrist, knot on the uppermost side. Pass the string through the horizontal hole on the controlling cross. With the puppet lying face up on the worksurface, place the hand with the string attached at the cuff position. Place the other hand next to the other cuff. Adjust the string length to that required and tie the loose end to the second hand. Hold knots in place at the wrists using

instant glue. Trim the loose ends.
❻ Insert the hand ball into the appropriate sleeve and pull the gathering tight. Tie off and cut the loose ends. Repeat for the other hand and for both boots.
❼ Attach the top ends of the strings to the controlling cross, ensuring that, when the controlling cross is horizontal and the puppet is standing, that all the strings are tight from cross to body part. Trim off loose ends.
Your clown is now ready to perform! ●

Jeff Loader's woodworking career led him to set up and run a wooden-toy-making workshop. This not only involved design and manufacture, but also the instruction of novices in various workshop practices and methods. Through this work he soon realized the love and joy of making, and playing with, wooden toys.

Jeff has written articles for various woodworking and modelling publications, as well as co-writing Making Board, Peg and Dice Games (GMC Publications Ltd) with his partner, Jennie.

Wooden toys and games apart, Jeff's many interests and activities include furniture design, restoring and using old woodworking tools, sport and playing (coping?!) with his young family.

Jennie Loader has a keen and active interest in many aspects of art, craft and design. She has studied photography and Leisure Management. To date her career has revolved around organizing drama, creative play, sporting and other pastime activities for varying groups of children, including those with special needs.

Jeff and Jennie were both born in the West Country and now live in Glastonbury with their two young children.

SPITFIRE and messerschmitt 109

These two representatives of the Battle of Britain are approximately ¼th scale. I have taken some liberties with the proportions but kept the characteristics of each machine. Both aeroplanes are identical in construction apart from some minor details.

The main tool required is a fretsaw followed by a drill, Stanley knife and various grades of glasspaper.

Construction

❶ Cut out all the parts before assembly as shown in photo 1. Prepare the wooden wheels by countersinking the hole in them to accept the countersink screw head.

Take care when cutting out the fuselage parts to ensure there is a slot for the propeller shaft (fig 1) and for the undercarriage on the 12mm centre section.

All the parts cut out

Join together two pieces of 6mm ply with double sided tape and cut out the side sections. These are the same as the centre but minus the U/C and propeller slots, fin and rudder and

The inability to find Spitfire and Messerschmitt models to stand up to a young boy's enthusiastic play prompts Ivor Carlyle to come to the rescue

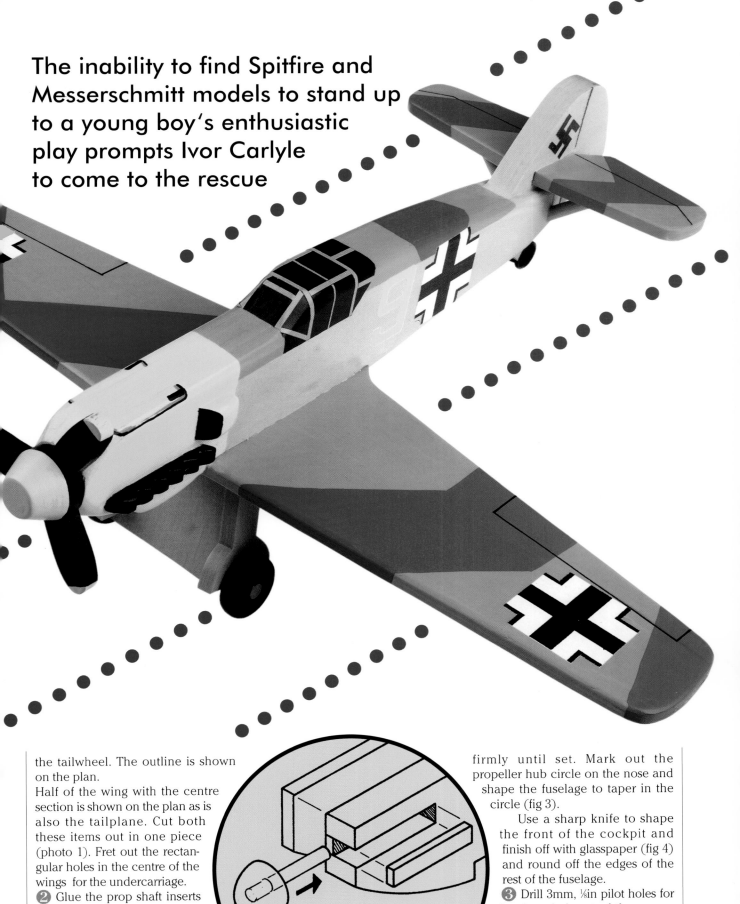

Fig 1

the tailwheel. The outline is shown on the plan.

Half of the wing with the centre section is shown on the plan as is also the tailplane. Cut both these items out in one piece (photo 1). Fret out the rectangular holes in the centre of the wings for the undercarriage.

② Glue the prop shaft inserts into the centre section (fig 1) and allow to set. Before gluing the sides on, taper the rear ends (fig 2) with a sanding block. Tape or temporarily pin the sides into position while gluing and clamp firmly until set. Mark out the propeller hub circle on the nose and shape the fuselage to taper in the circle (fig 3).

Use a sharp knife to shape the front of the cockpit and finish off with glasspaper (fig 4) and round off the edges of the rest of the fuselage.

③ Drill 3mm, ⅛in pilot holes for the threaded part of the screws into the axle stubs before assembling. This is important in order to avoid splitting the ply when fitting the screws. Glue the undercarriage flaps onto the sides of the U/C axle. Note

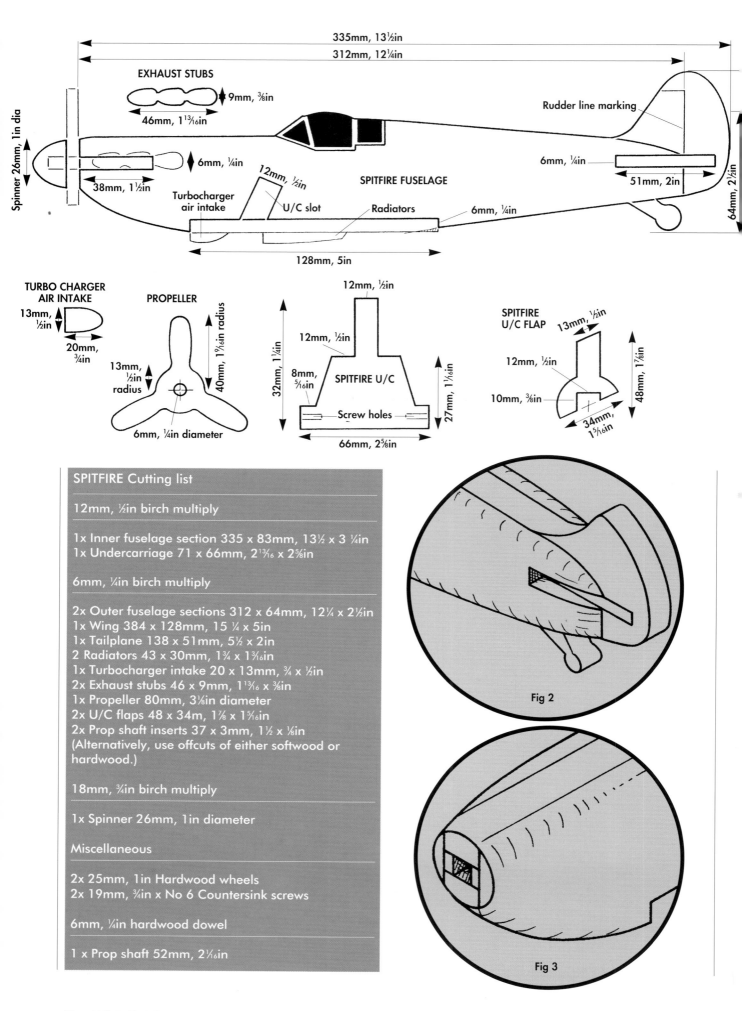

335mm, 13½in

312mm, 12¼in

EXHAUST STUBS

9mm, ⅜in

46mm, 1¹³⁄₁₆in

Rudder line marking

Spinner 26mm, 1in dia

6mm, ¼in

6mm, ¼in

38mm, 1½in

51mm, 2in

64mm, 2½in

Turbocharger
air intake

12mm, ½in

U/C slot

Radiators

6mm, ¼in

SPITFIRE FUSELAGE

128mm, 5in

**TURBO CHARGER
AIR INTAKE**

13mm,
½in

20mm,
¾in

PROPELLER

40mm, 1⁹⁄₁₆in radius

13mm,
½in
radius

6mm, ¼in diameter

12mm, ½in

12mm, ½in

32mm, 1¼in

8mm,
⁵⁄₁₆in

SPITFIRE U/C

27mm, 1¹⁄₁₆in

Screw holes

66mm, 2⅝in

**SPITFIRE
U/C FLAP**

13mm, ½in

12mm, ½in

10mm, ⅜in

48mm, 1⅞in

34mm,
1⁵⁄₁₆in

SPITFIRE Cutting list

12mm, ½in birch multiply

1x Inner fuselage section 335 x 83mm, 13½ x 3 ¼in
1x Undercarriage 71 x 66mm, 2¹³⁄₁₆ x 2⅝in

6mm, ¼in birch multiply

2x Outer fuselage sections 312 x 64mm, 12¼ x 2½in
1x Wing 384 x 128mm, 15 ¼ x 5in
1x Tailplane 138 x 51mm, 5½ x 2in
2 Radiators 43 x 30mm, 1¾ x 1³⁄₁₆in
1x Turbocharger intake 20 x 13mm, ¾ x ½in
2x Exhaust stubs 46 x 9mm, 1¹³⁄₁₆ x ⅜in
1x Propeller 80mm, 3⅛in diameter
2x U/C flaps 48 x 34m, 1⅞ x 1⁵⁄₁₆in
2x Prop shaft inserts 37 x 3mm, 1½ x ⅛in
(Alternatively, use offcuts of either softwood or
hardwood.)

18mm, ¾in birch multiply

1x Spinner 26mm, 1in diameter

Miscellaneous

2x 25mm, 1in Hardwood wheels
2x 19mm, ¾in x No 6 Countersink screws

6mm, ¼in hardwood dowel

1 x Prop shaft 52mm, 2¹⁄₁₆in

Fig 2

Fig 3

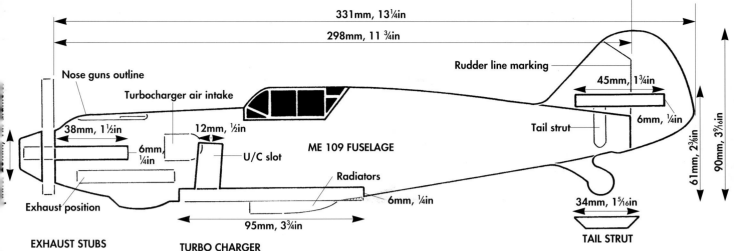

331mm, 13¼in

298mm, 11 ¾in

Rudder line marking

45mm, 1¾in

Nose guns outline

Turbocharger air intake

38mm, 1½in

12mm, ½in

6mm, ¼in

Tail strut

6mm, ¼in

U/C slot

ME 109 FUSELAGE

90mm, 3⅝in

61mm, 2⅜in

Radiators

Exhaust position

6mm, ¼in

34mm, 1⁵⁄₁₆in

95mm, 3¾in

TAIL STRUT

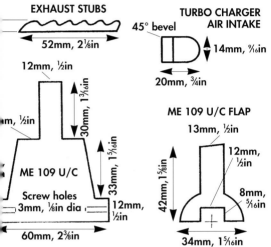

EXHAUST STUBS

52mm, 2⅛in

TURBO CHARGER AIR INTAKE

45° bevel

14mm, ⁹⁄₁₆in

20mm, ¾in

12mm, ½in

30mm, 1³⁄₁₆in

ME 109 U/C FLAP

13mm, ½in

12mm, ½in

m, ½in

33mm, 1⁵⁄₁₆in

42mm, 1⅝in

8mm, ⁵⁄₁₆in

ME 109 U/C

Screw holes

3mm, ⅛in dia

12mm, ½in

60mm, 2⅜in

34mm, 1⁵⁄₁₆in

how the notch in the flap sits on the axle stub. The flaps on the Spitfire will protrude beyond the axle stubs so rub down this part with glasspaper until it is flush.

④ Taper with glasspaper the undersurface of the centre section of the wing where it protrudes away from the fuselage. When this has been done, glue the wing into position while using the U/C assembly to ensure the hole in

the wing aligns with the slot in the fuselage. Fix temporarily with two pins and remove the U/C. Glue also the tailplane into place. Round off all the edges of the wings and tailplane.

⑤ Glue the prop shaft into the 6mm, ¼in hole in the prop spinner and shape the spinner with glasspaper using the shaft as a handle. (Should you have a lathe this will make shaping the spinners and wheels easier. Alternatively a drill press or horizontally-mounted power drill can also be pressed into service. – Ed)

MESSERSCHMITT 109 Cutting list

12mm birch multiply

1x Inner fuselage section 331 x 90mm, 13¼ x 3⁹⁄₁₆in
1x Undercarriage 75 x 60mm, 3 x 2⅜in
1x Spinner 26 mm, 1in diameter

6mm, ¼in birch multiply

2 x Outer fuselage sections 298 x 61mm, 11¾ x 2⅜in
1x Wing 372 x 95mm, 14⅝ x 3¾in
1x Tailplane 138 x 45mm, 5½ x 1¾in
2x Radiators 45 x 30mm, 1¹³⁄₁₆ x 1³⁄₁₆in
1x Turbocharger intake 20 x 14mm, ¾ x ⁹⁄₁₆in
2x Exhaust stubs 52 x 6mm, 2⅛ x ¼in
1x Propeller 80mm, 3⅛in diameter
2x U/C flaps 42 x 34mm, 1⅝ x 1⁵⁄₁₆in
2x Prop shaft inserts 37 x 3mm, 1½ x ⅛in

Miscellaneous

2 x 25mm, 1in Hardwood wheels
2x 19mm, ¾in x No 6 Countersink screws

6mm, ¼in Hardwood dowel

1x Prop shaft 52mm, 2¹⁄₁₆in
2x Tail struts 45mm, 1¾in

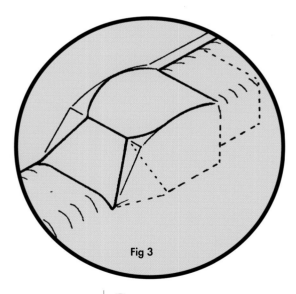

Fig 3

⑥ Shape the underwing radiators to the profiles shown on the fuselage side views with a sanding block, rounding off the sharp corners and edges. Repeat with turbocharger intakes and the exhaust stubs . Glue into their positions as shown on the plans.
⑦ Glue the tail support struts for the ME 109 into position shown on the plane.
⑧ Do not assemble the propeller assembly or attach the wheels until painting is complete.

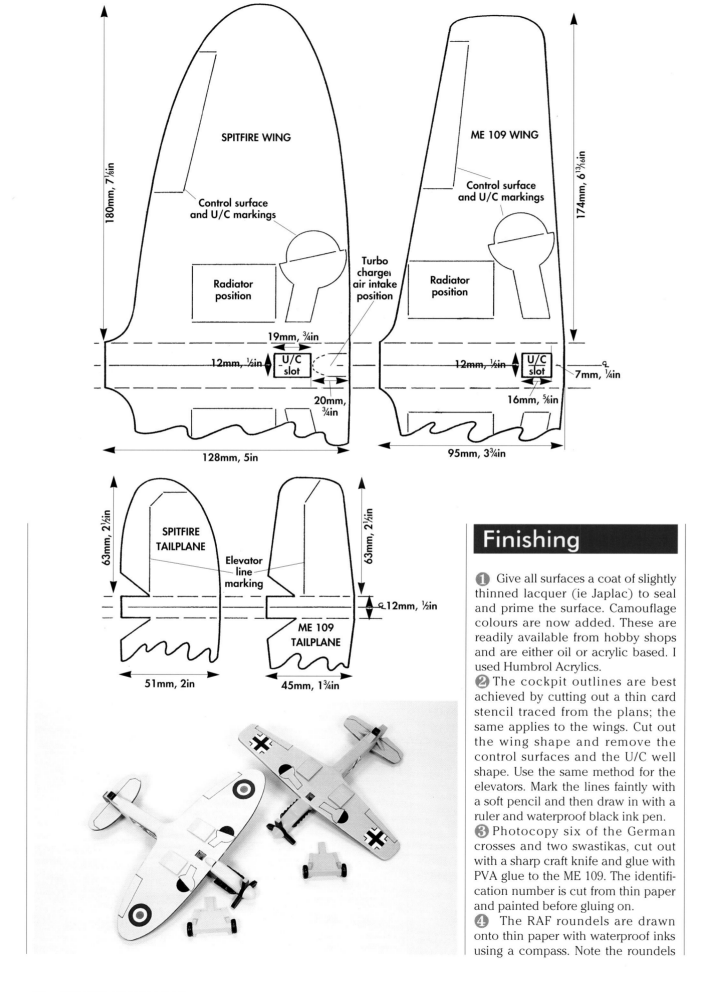

SPITFIRE WING

ME 109 WING

Control surface
and U/C markings

Control surface
and U/C markings

180mm, 7⅛in

174mm, 6¹³⁄₁₆in

Radiator
position

Radiator
position

Turbo
charger
air intake
position

19mm, ¾in

12mm, ½in

U/C
slot

12mm, ½in

U/C
slot

7mm, ¼in

20mm,
¾in

16mm, ⅝in

128mm, 5in

95mm, 3¾in

63mm, 2½in

SPITFIRE
TAILPLANE

Elevator
line
marking

63mm, 2½in

12mm, ½in

ME 109
TAILPLANE

51mm, 2in

45mm, 1¾in

Finishing

❶ Give all surfaces a coat of slightly thinned lacquer (ie Japlac) to seal and prime the surface. Camouflage colours are now added. These are readily available from hobby shops and are either oil or acrylic based. I used Humbrol Acrylics.

❷ The cockpit outlines are best achieved by cutting out a thin card stencil traced from the plans; the same applies to the wings. Cut out the wing shape and remove the control surfaces and the U/C well shape. Use the same method for the elevators. Mark the lines faintly with a soft pencil and then draw in with a ruler and waterproof black ink pen.

❸ Photocopy six of the German crosses and two swastikas, cut out with a sharp craft knife and glue with PVA glue to the ME 109. The identification number is cut from thin paper and painted before gluing on.

❹ The RAF roundels are drawn onto thin paper with waterproof inks using a compass. Note the roundels

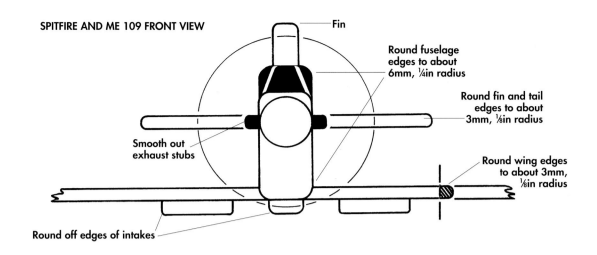

SPITFIRE AND ME 109 FRONT VIEW

Fin

Round fuselage edges to about 6mm, ¼in radius

Round fin and tail edges to about 3mm, ⅛in radius

Smooth out exhaust stubs

Round wing edges to about 3mm, ⅛in radius

Round off edges of intakes

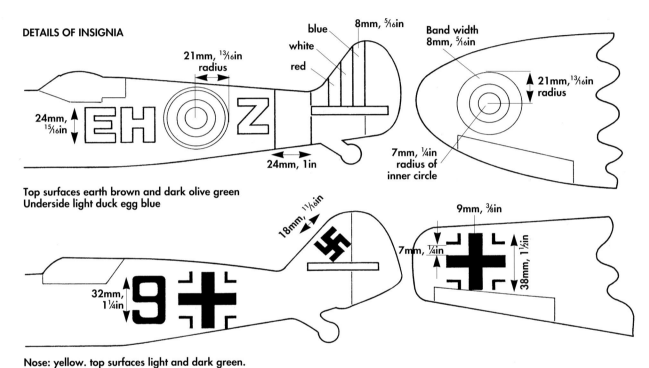

DETAILS OF INSIGNIA

21mm, ¹³⁄₁₆in radius

24mm, ¹⁵⁄₁₆in

24mm, 1in

blue
white
red

8mm, ⁵⁄₁₆in

Band width 8mm, ⁵⁄₁₆in

21mm, ¹³⁄₁₆in radius

7mm, ¼in radius of inner circle

Top surfaces earth brown and dark olive green
Underside light duck egg blue

18mm, ¹¹⁄₁₆in

32mm, 1¼in

9mm, ⅜in

7mm, ¼in

38mm, 1½in

Nose: yellow. top surfaces light and dark green.
All other areas light grey

on top of the wing are blue and red, underneath blue, white and red, and those on the fuselage have a thin yellow border.

5 The squadron markings are cut from thin paper also. The cockpit frame work is made by cutting 2mm, (¹⁄₁₆in) strips from pre-painted paper that has been backed with doubled sided tape. Use a really sharp scalpel type craft knife for this.

6 I finally gave everything two coats of Rustins matt acrylic varnish, which is almost colourless.

7 The U/C can be left to detach for retracted appearance while in 'flight'. The propshaft is glued into the propshaft slot leaving the propeller free to rotate.

8 Attach the wheels with the screws, and cover the screw heads with prepainted paper backed with doubled sided tape and punched out into discs with a stationery punch.

AUTHOR'S NOTE

Some people may be offended at the inclusion of the swastika on a toy. This was the standard marking on German aircraft during the Second World War and this feature has made a useful talking point for explaining to younger people what it stood for. The appalling fate that would have overcome us if the RAF hadn't defeated the Luftwaffe during the Battle of Britain is worth the retelling. ●

Ivor Carlyle works full time as an illustrator and model maker, covering diverse subjects such as a working model watermill to puppet heads and props for advertising photography. An increasing number of nephews and nieces prompted an interest in producing quick and easy-to-make toys.

ZINDERNEUF

This Beau Geste-style fort by Terry Lawrence will capture the imagination of boys of all ages

FORT
zinderneuf

hose of you who have read the book 'Beau Geste', or seen the film starring Gary Cooper, will know what to expect: a white fort in the Sahara desert, housing members of the French Foreign Legion. Situated near an oasis, yet not preventing the Bedouin access to water, it is surprisingly small, because all the materials to build and equip it have had to be hauled by men and animals across the pitiless desert.

I have made the construction of this version very simple. There are no joints to cut; the walls are held together with standard plastic assembly blocks, and all interior detail is freestanding. The removal of four bolts will dismantle the whole thing for easy storage. All the cutting can be done on the smallest scroll saw (fretsaw) – or with hand saws if you prefer.

There are, in fact, two versions: the basic unit is quick to construct, as it comprises four walls, baseboard, walkway and tower; about four to five hours in the workshop. The second version is as above, but includes lots of extra detail, all simple to make, and from which you can select whatever elements you and your child want.

The fort is cheap to make. Most of it can be made from MDF (medium density fibreboard), and the basic version of the fort will cost only about £11. Adding the interior details is more a matter of time than material costs, but as photographed, the top o' the range edition will cost you about £15.

The scale is at ¼in to 1ft (1:48 scale). The top of the crenellation is 1½in (38mm) (representing 6ft /1800mm) above the walkway, so a soldier is protected from rifle fire. If your model soldiers are to a different scale, just enlarge (by photocopier) the magazine drawings accordingly.

Construction notes

Walls

❶ East and west walls are identical, and each is cut from ½in (12mm) MDF, 5in wide and 18in long 125 x 460mm). This material is cheap to buy, easy to work, and more resistant to warping than plywood or solid timber.

❷ Cut the two pieces to these dimensions, and mark out, with try-square and pencil, the crenellations at the top edge. All crenellation (crenels are the solid bits, and voids are the spaces between) is ½in (12mm) deep and ⅜in (10mm) wide. The proportions of the walls are

Cutting list	
Walls:	12mm (½in) MDF: 450 x 560mm (18in x 22in)
Staircases and armoury:	3in x ¾in: 4ft 6in (75 x 19mm x 1350mm)
Tower and baseboard:	6mm (¼in) MDF: 14in x 28in (355 x 710mm)
Walkway and stable roof:	1½in x ¼in timber : 6ft 6in (38 x 6mm x 1980mm)
Baseboard surface:	cork sheet 1mm thick: 14in x 18in (355 x 460mm)
Arches and spacers:	3in x 1in timber: 14in (75 x 25mm x 355mm)
Fixings:	4prs white plastic assembly blocks
Doors, water barrels etc,	from scrap

The four fort walls, with assembly blocks attached

Walls assembled, with gateway stones in place

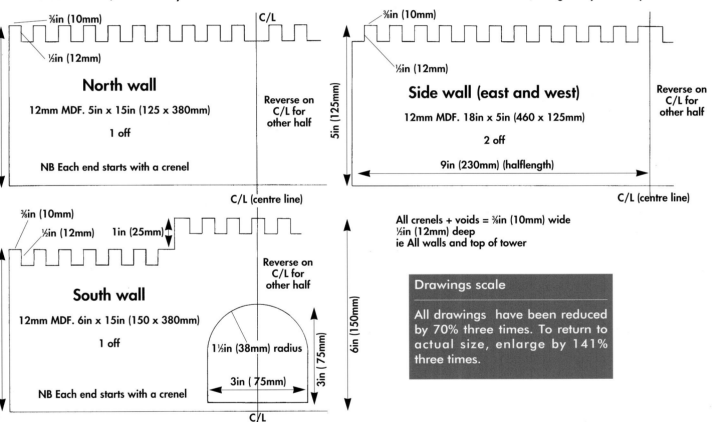

North wall

⅜in (10mm)

½in (12mm)

C/L

12mm MDF. 5in x 15in (125 x 380mm)

1 off

NB Each end starts with a crenel

Reverse on C/L for other half

C/L (centre line)

Side wall (east and west)

⅜in (10mm)

½in (12mm)

5in (125mm)

12mm MDF. 18in x 5in (460 x 125mm)

2 off

9in (230mm) (halflength)

Reverse on C/L for other half

C/L (centre line)

South wall

⅜in (10mm)

½in (12mm)

1in (25mm)

12mm MDF. 6in x 15in (150 x 380mm)

1 off

NB Each end starts with a crenel

Reverse on C/L for other half

1½in (38mm) radius

3in (75mm)

3in (75mm)

6in (150mm)

C/L

All crenels + voids = ⅜in (10mm) wide
½in (12mm) deep
ie All walls and top of tower

Drawings scale

All drawings have been reduced by 70% three times. To return to actual size, enlarge by 141% three times.

such that there is a wide crenel at the centre of each long wall, so you should mark from each end in toward the centre, starting with a void. If it is important to you to achieve uniformity, you can shorten each wall by ⅜in (10mm) and adjust the baseboard and interior fittings accordingly.

❸ The two short walls (north and south) are both 15in (380mm) long. The north wall is again 5in (125mm) high, matching the side walls, but the south wall differs, in that it has a

raised centre section 1in (25mm) higher, above the arched 3in x 3in (75 x 75mm) cut-out for the main gates.

❹ Points to note are that both short walls again are marked for cutting the crenellation from each end in toward the centre, and both have crenels at each end, not voids. The cut-out for the gates is straight-forward, but just note that its base is 7mm above the base edge. This thickness exactly matches the baseboard which will sit inside the

walls after assembly (6mm MDF baseboard, covered with 1mm thick cork sheet, which you can buy from

NOTE In the author's original manuscript the dimensions were given in imperial but, for the convenience of readers, we give dimensions in both imperial and metric. However, if you are using metric do check the measurements carefully, as the conversion is approximate.

a model railway stockist).

5 You may now fix the four pairs of assembly blocks. Use ⅝in (15mm) No 6 chipboard screws, which will not penetrate the MDF. Mark and drill pilot holes for the screws. The blocks, an assembled pair of which measure 1½in x 1⅛in x ½in (38 x 30 x 12mm), should be mounted as shown in the photo, so that when the four walls are assembled, the bolts of the blocks run north/south, parallel with the staircases which hide them.

Base

1 Leave the four walls assembled. Check the corners for squareness (90°), place over a sheet of 6mm MDF, and draw all round inside the walls. Cut out the baseboard so marked, and check for fit. Cut a piece of cork sheet, a little oversize. Apply white PVA glue to the baseboard, lay on the cork sheet, and reverse onto a flat surface covered with kitchen clingfilm (in case any glue squeezes out). Place weights on top. Check after ten minutes that there are no bubbles of air under the cork: if there are, just slash them with a scalpel and press down. Replace the board inverted, with weights on top, and leave overnight to dry. You can then trim the cork sheet to match the MDF and place the baseboard in position within the walls.

2 You can now start to make the interior fittings. Leave all painting until you have finished construction of all the elements you want.

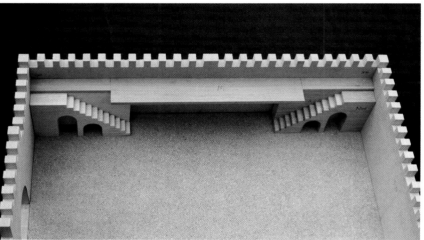

Staircase

Photo 3 shows one of the staircases, which comprises two pieces, each 3in (75mm) high and 5in (125mm) long. The backing piece is plain, with just a cut-out to accept and hide the assembly block. The front stepped piece takes a little longer to cut, but is straightforward, with treads and risers both ¼in (6mm).

Top **Staircase, with backing piece to hide block**
Above **Inside west wall: two staircases with walkway**

These two elements, when glued together, are exactly 1½in (38mm) thick, to match the width of the walkway all round the fort. Make four sets of staircases, all of which run north/south. Check for fit and correct glue side before gluing the pairs together. The pairs will be freestanding, so don't glue the staircases to the walls.

Walkway

This is 1½in (38mm) wide, cut from ¼in (6mm) thick wood. I used Vitex Cofassus, a useful close-grained wood from Papua New Guinea, but you can use 6mm MDF if you wish. If

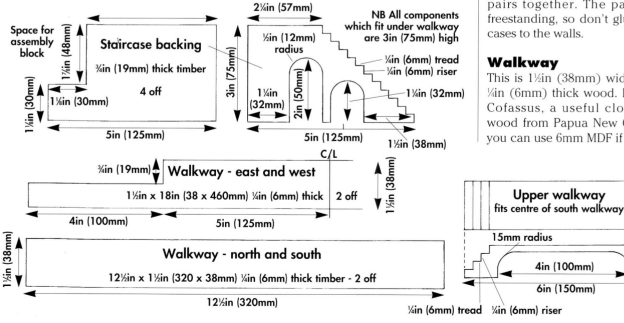

you construct some, at least, of the interior extras, the walkway will be supported and will not tilt or sag.

Note the 4in x ¾in (100 x 19mm) cut-outs at each end of the long strips. These are required to give access from the staircase to the walkway, and also to provide headroom for the Legionnaires as they ascend. Cut the raised 1in (25mm) high upper walkway from 1½in (38mm) thick timber, and place it in position above the gateway.

Tower

❶ This unit, at 10in (250mm), is just twice the height of the main walls. Cut the four sides from 6mm (¼in) MDF. All four are identical in length and width, with crenellation the same size as that of the walls. All four have crenels at each end of the top edge. Cut two 1in (25mm) square holes in each of two sides, to accept window frames later, and cut out, as shown on the drawing, a centre recess on the top of one side, above where the external ladder will be fitted.

❷ Now cut two formers of ½in (12mm) or thicker softwood. As the drawing shows, one former is located at the base of the tower, and the other with its top surface 1½in (38mm)

Below **Fitting the window frames to tower**
Bottom **Inserting the tower ladder rungs**

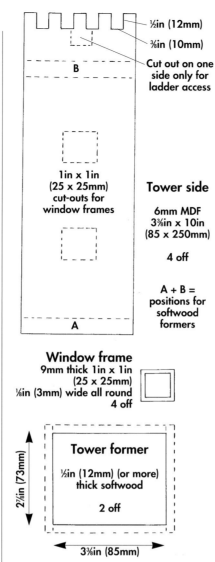

½in (12mm)
⅜in (10mm)
Cut out on one side only for ladder access

B

1in x 1in (25 x 25mm) cut-outs for window frames

Tower side

6mm MDF
3⅜in x 10in (85 x 250mm)

4 off

A + B = positions for softwood formers

A

Window frame
9mm thick 1in x 1in (25 x 25mm)
⅛in (3mm) wide all round
4 off

Tower former
½in (12mm) (or more) thick softwood
2 off

2⅞in (73mm)

3⅜in (85mm)

Positions of the four tower walls

below the top of the crenellation. The pieces are oblong, so that one pair of sides overlaps the other pair.

❸ Pin and glue the two tower sides with window apertures to the 3⅜in (85mm) sides of the formers (I used ½in, 12mm panel pins and white PVA glue). Apply glue to the long edges of these sides, then pin and glue the other two sides, and leave to dry.

❹ The assembly at this stage is stark and rather ugly; it needs to be improved a little. I have done this with projecting window frames and an external ladder. Cut four window frames from 9mm thick timber. They should be 1in (25mm) square externally, to fit the cut apertures in two of the tower sides, and the frame width should be ⅛in (3mm). Glue these into place, and they will be 3mm proud of the tower wall surface.

❺ For the external ladder (which you will see in the Gary Cooper film) cut two pieces of wood ³⁄₁₆in x ¼in (5 x 6mm) section and 9in (230mm) long. Sand and place together so the ¼in (6mm) sides touch, and hold together with a couple of bits of masking tape. Mark the length at ¼in (6mm) intervals and drill ¹⁄₁₆in (1.5mm drill bit) right through the pair at each marked station. This provides matching holes for the rungs.

❻ Glue the two strips, by their ³⁄₁₆in (5mm) sides, onto the tower wall with a cut-out on top, so that the finished ladder width is ¾in (19mm). When the glue is dry, you can paint the tower white, including the area between the ladder stiles. I used ordinary household vinyl emulsion, but you may prefer a satin finish, which can be more easily wiped free of dirty fingerprints!

❼ When dry, you can add the rungs to the ladder. These are ¾in (19mm) lengths of cocktail sticks, and are most easily fitted by pushing the stick right through a pair of holes, then cutting off flush with the outside edge of the stiles, with scalpel or craft saw (see photo).

❽ When all are in position, paint the outside edges of the ladder again with more white emulsion, which will glue the rungs in place. If necessary, scrape the long outside face of the ladder stiles with a scalpel or other sharp blade to remove any excess paint.

❾ Paint a tricolour flag on white card, mount on a length of 5mm

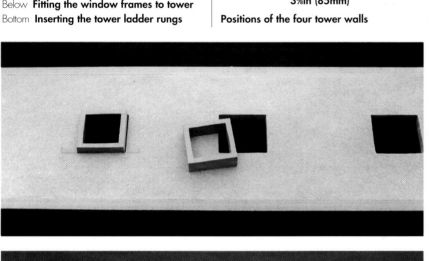

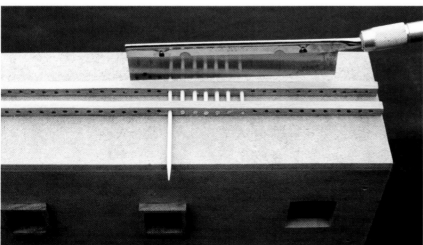

dowel (just bisect the top 1in/25mm with the finest scroll saw blade) and fix in a 5mm hole drilled in the top tower former. If you are worried that your child may fall on the flagstaff and be injured, then just make the dowel of balsa wood, which will break under any load.

That completes the work for the basic Fort Zinderneuf. Now I will describe the little extras which personalise and add interest to the basic design. All of these items are very simple and cheap to make.

Gates

❶ First let me say that you can use commercial hinges for the gates if you wish. However, I chose to make my own hinges, from ¼in (6mm) square strip wood, glued to the gates' inside face and the south wall's inner

face. As the photos show, removable brass wire hinge pins fit in holes drilled in the strips.

❷ The gates were cut from a scrap piece of hardwood (in this case, Masasa from Zimbabwe) ½in (12mm) thick, with the grain vertical. You can use the MDF cut-out from the wall as a template if you wish.

❸ When you have made the vertical cut which turns this shape into two gates, cut 5mm wide strips of veneer (of matching, or contrasting, wood). I used mahogany, with the grain horizontal. Cut these strips and glue to the front face of the gates, trimming each end. Cut some ¼in (6mm) square timber, to the lengths indicated in the drawing, together

Below **Exterior of gateway**
Bottom **Interior of gateway**

with matching stubs which will be glued to the wall as bearers. Mark and drill ¹⁄₁₆in (1.5mm) vertical holes in all pieces for the hinge pins. Cut 2in (50mm) lengths of 1mm brass rod (or use long panel pins or nails) and check the fit before gluing the assembly, leaving the pins in place, parallel with the vertical edge of the gates to ensure alignment.

❹ When the glue is set, remove the gates by lifting out the two hinge pins, and chamfer the centre vertical edges of the gates about 3° inward, to allow them to open freely. This is because the pivot point is behind the centre of the gate thickness.

❺ Remove the south wall from the fort, and place flat with the outer face upward. You may now cut, from 2–3mm thick timber, random stone shapes, and glue them around the gateway, trimming to the curve after the glue is set.

❻ Cut a piece of the same timber approximately 3in x ½in (75 x 12mm) for the name-plate. Place it in the desired position above the gateway, and mark its position (and don't paint that little oblong). Paint the strip white, and when dry, you can affix the name. I used Edding 7.5mm self-adhesive lettering, but you could use Letraset or similar dry transfer if you wish.

Stable

❶ This is the little structure shown inside the East wall, with a projecting strung roof. It stables horses or camels (Britain's models are in scale at 2in/50mm high, but you need a single humped camel, not a dromedary, which is Asian). You can fit a tethering bar (5mm dowel) during assembly if you wish. **The strung roof is to support palm fronds from the oasis, to give shade to the animals.**

❷ The back and side pieces are simply pinned and glued together, then slid under the walkway, which then forms part of the roofing. Drill small holes at each end of the shade piece, which is cut from the same timber as the walkway. Now you can string with twine or thin string.

❸ To achieve a little tension and avoid sag, apply superglue with a cocktail stick into one end hole. Pass the string through the hole from the inside of the frame, and secure by pushing the glued point of the stick into the hole from the outside,

Main Gate
½in (12mm) thick timber

5mm wide viewer strips

Exterior   Interior

¼in (6mm) square strip

3in (75mm)

3in (75mm)

drilled 1.5mm for hinge pin

ZINDERNEUF

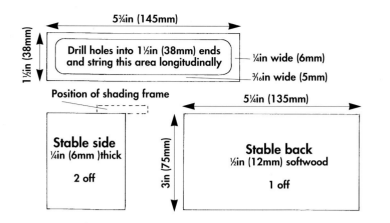

5¾in (145mm)

1½in (38mm)

Drill holes into 1½in (38mm) ends and string this area longitudinally

¼in wide (6mm)

³⁄₁₆in wide (5mm)

Position of shading frame

Stable side
¼in (6mm)thick

2 off

3in (75mm)

5¼in (135mm)

Stable back
½in (12mm) softwood

1 off

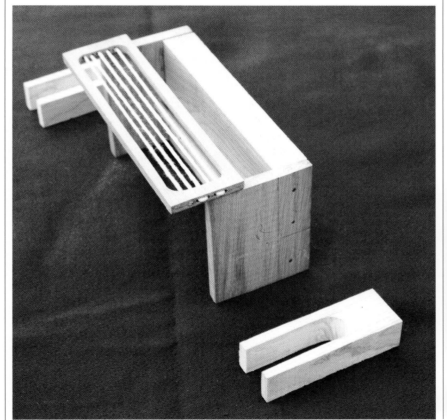

Above **Stable assembly with niche spacers**

alongside the string end.

❹ When the glue has set, cut off excess stick and string. Cut the string to leave about 3ft (900mm), and dip the free end into superglue, to form a hard point, and thread through the other holes, anchoring the end as before. Glue the finished shade into place on the tops of the side walls, abutting the walkway.

❺ Cut spacer pieces from 1in or 1¼in (25 or 32mm) thick softwood, with little arched cut-outs, to fit either side of the stable, between it and the staircases. **This makes little niches, for any Legionnaire waiting to ascend the staircase.**

Barrack Block

❶ This is of similar construction to the stable, but has a solid removable roof, and a front wall with windows and door. The unit fits under the walkway, which provides one third of its roofing. I have left the apertures unfilled, but you can, if you wish, add a little hinged door. You can also make little roller blinds for the windows, cut from split bamboo table matting (the type where the strands of bamboo are stitched together; stop the thread running by applying a dab of superglue before cutting).

❷ You can also make little beds and cupboards for the interior. The roof is just two strips of walkway timber glued together along the edges, with a ¼in (6mm) strip rim on top, and a ¼in (6mm) strip locator underneath.

Below **Barrack block with roof removed**
Bottom **Looking north: barrack and ablutions in place**

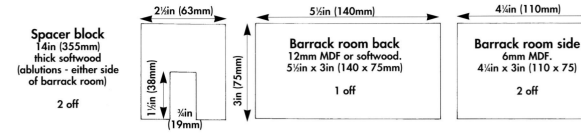

Spacer block
14in (355mm)
thick softwood
(ablutions - either side
of barrack room)

2 off

2½in (63mm)

1½in (38mm)   ¾in (19mm)

3in (75mm)

Barrack room back
12mm MDF or softwood.
5½in x 3in (140 x 75mm)

1 off

5½in (140mm)

Barrack room side
6mm MDF.
4¼in x 3in (110 x 75)

2 off

4¼in (110mm)

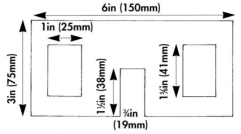

6in (150mm)

1in (25mm)

3in (75mm)

1½in (38mm)   ¾in (19mm)

1⅝in (41mm)

Barrack room front wall
6mm wood. 6in x 3in (150 x 75mm) 1 off

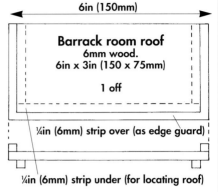

6in (150mm)

Barrack room roof
6mm wood.
6in x 3in (150 x 75mm)

1 off

¼in (6mm) strip over (as edge guard)

¼in (6mm) strip under (for locating roof)

❸ Now cut, from 1¼in (32mm) thick timber, spacer pieces to fit between barrack block and staircases. These pieces have doorways cut, to represent ablution rooms.

Armoury

The armoury is the unit inside the West wall, and is partly hidden,

Looking west: Armoury in place

when the tower is located adjacent to it. It is very simple to make, and comprises just two pieces of timber ¾in (19mm) thick and 3in (75mm) high. The rear piece has arches cut at each end (to match the spacers either side of the stable opposite). The front piece has a doorway, offset to the left, so that it is not blocked by the tower. After checking the fit, between staircases, of the rear piece, glue the two together. The front face will match the edge of the walkway.

Storage Arches

These are two identical pieces, cut from 1¼in (32mm) thick timber, and which stand inside the South wall on either side of the gates, and abutting the South staircases. They provide storage space for water casks, of which you see four in the photos. **These barrels were checked daily, and replenished from the oasis.**

Emergency water barrel
4 off

1½in (38mm)

1in (25mm)
dia

The barrels are turned from 1in (25mm) dia oak. I cheated by using English oak, though the real ones would have been made of French Limousin oak. I defy you to spot the difference! The photo shows the

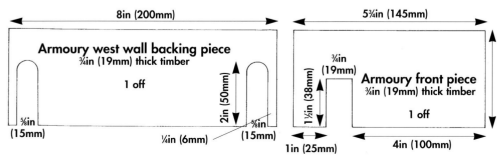

8in (200mm)

Armoury west wall backing piece
¾in (19mm) thick timber

1 off

⅝in (15mm)

2in (50mm)

⅝in (15mm)

¼in (6mm)

5¾in (145mm)

¾in (19mm)

Armoury front piece
¾in (19mm) thick timber

1 off

1½in (38mm)

1in (25mm)   4in (100mm)

Left **Turning the water barrels: the four stages**
Below **Looking south: arches and barrels in place**
Right **Basic unpainted components assembled**
Bottom **Interior components, painted**

four stages of turning: 1½in (38mm) length delineated with a parting tool; basic shape achieved with ⅜in (10mm) gouge and square ended scraper; barrel hoops marked and cut with parting tool; hoops coloured with black felt-tip pen, whilst rotating the lathe by hand. (If you try to colour with the lathe turning, the pen cannot feed ink to its tip quickly enough.)

Painting

The photos show clearly the faces of each component to be painted. The walls and tower took two coats of vinyl emulsion; the painted faces of the interior piece took only one coat. Keep the painted pieces off the cork baseboard until dry. The final touch is to glue in place above the main gate, the "Zinderneuf" name-plate. ●

Terry Lawrence started making toys over thirty years ago, when his two sets of twins were young. As a low-paid Civil Servant, he couldn't afford shop-bought toys (nothing much has changed!). He soon found that what he made was better than the commercially-produced variety, and his children had more fun with them. In addition, there was great satisfaction in making individual designs for his own family. Terry's designs now appear regularly in the magazines *Woodturning* and *The Woodworker*. His book *Turning Wooden Toys* has been published by GMC Publications Ltd, and includes projects ranging from a simple set of Colourmix spinning tops, to his version of Jules Verne's submarine "Nautilus", with oval-turned hull.

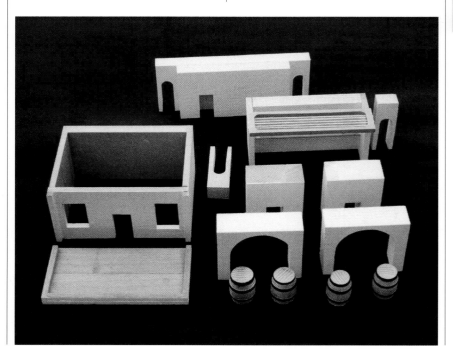

Rock around
the clock

Made from ply and MDF, these simple rocking toys by
Roy Anderson *will keep everyone amused*

**Fig. 1 Full-size template
Chicken (one piece of ply)**

120 (4³⁄4")

160 (6¹⁄4")

100 (4") dia

Not to be stained or painted

Materials required
- 3mm (¹⁄8") birch ply, 610mm x 915mm (24" x 36")
- MDF (medium-density fibre board) 300mm x 610mm x 12mm thick (12" x 24" x ¹⁄2" thick)
- Acrylic or Pelikan Plaka paint (assorted colours)
- Clear interior gloss varnish
- Rustin's Colorglaze stains: yellow, blue, green and red
- Gloss toy paints with primer and undercoat (various colours)
- Brushes: 2 small bristle brushes for staining and varnishing; sable artists' brushes for details

Preparing ply for toys

1 Four sheets of 3mm (¹⁄8in) ply, 180mm x 230mm (6in x 9in) are stained with three coats of Rustin's Colorglaze stain: yellow, blue, green and red. Do not stain each figure's half-circle ply base as this will be glued to the MDF rockers. The shades of colour can be your own choice as all stains are intermixable and non-toxic. The last coat is sanded slightly as clear varnish is applied later.

Note: Both sides of the ply figures are stained. Apply masking tape over the half-circle ply base as this section should not be stained or painted.

Tracing figures onto ply

1 Lay a sheet of tracing paper over the full-size figure or enlarge as illustrated. Use a hard 'H' or '2H' pencil to outline the details of each figure.

2 Then rub a soft pencil, 'B' or '2B', over the outlines you have drawn, but on the reverse side of the tracing paper. Turn back to the front side of the tracing paper and now re-trace the figure onto the stained ply with a hard 'H' or '2H' pencil. This method will imprint the lines onto the ply.
Note: Carbon paper can also be used.

Cutting out & painting
1 Cut out the figures in one complete piece including the half-circle bases with a fretsaw. The details on the figures can be painted with acrylic or Pelikan Plaka colours.
2 The figures are then given a coat of gloss clear varnish to protect the paint and general rocking wear and tear.
Note: Do not varnish or paint the figure's half-circle ply base.

The rockers
1 These are cut out of MDF circles 100mm (4in) dia, 12mm (1/2in) thick as MDF is heavier than timber. The size is slightly larger than the half-circle of the ply figures. To get a good circle before cutting, a small nut and bolt is inserted through the centre of both circles and fixed onto a drill (pillar drill if possible), and the edges sanded.
2 The inside of both half-circles are not painted, but the outside and edges are painted in a gloss non-toxic paint. Use a primer for the first coat, then an undercoat, then a gloss coat and colour to your own choice.

Fixing rockers onto figures
1 Apply PVA to one side of each MDF half-circle. Insert the ply figure so that its base is sandwiched between the two MDF half-circles and cramp together the entire assembly until dry.

Suppliers
● W Hobby Ltd, Knights Hill Square, London, SE27 0HH. Tel: 0181-761-4244
● DIY stores and artists' merchants

Fig. 2 90% template Bandsman (one piece of ply)
110 (4¹/₄")

165 (6¹/₂")

100 (4") dia
Not to be stained or painted

Roy Anderson *was originally a signwriter with combined skills in poster writing and silk-screen printing. The great storm of 1987 in Britain provided more wood than usual and his interest in woodcarving took root. Roy's wife and son also became interested in automata which has proved to be "fascinating and educational".*

Fig. 3 50% template Harlequin (one piece of ply)
115 (4¹/₂")

170 (6³/₄")

100 (4") dia
Not to be stained or painted

Fig. 4 50% template Columbine (one piece of ply)
130 (5")

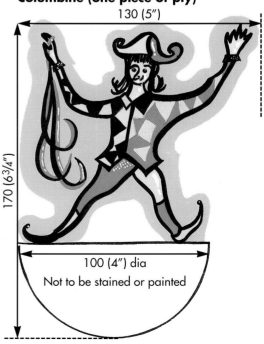

170 (6³/₄")

100 (4") dia
Not to be stained or painted

Ride-on lc

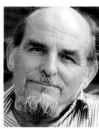

Rex Coleman *started his working life as an apprentice wood pattern maker. He joined the Royal Engineers as a regular soldier serving in Egypt and Cyprus and went into engineering after he was demobbed in 1953. His engineering career ended in 1988 when he had his first heart attack. In 1995 he took medical retirement, but still manages to make a few toys and continues to enjoy woodworking.*

Top right: Layout of chassis and axle packer.
Right: Side view of chassis showing steering column collar in position.

THE FIRST step of this delightful project is to cut all the parts required for the main assembly; most of them are from 19mm (3/4in) thick pine. MDF would also suffice.

Chassis

1 First you need Nos. l to 5. Cut No. l to the drawing. Do not forget to drill the steering shaft hole right through 28mm (1^1/8in) if you should decide to use a 25mm (1in) dia. Do not forget to drill all steering holes the same. Drill the axle stops and glue in.
2 Cut out the arc in wheel arch strips No. 3 at 89mm (3^1/2in) centres from the rear edge and 89mm (3^1/2in) radius 12mm (1/2in) deep. Also cut out 19mm (3/4in) square from the front outer corner.
3 Get the two side members (No. 2) and drill three holes to take screws to affix to No. 3, keeping the top edges flush, as this will form the cargo floor.
4 Drill through the 19mm (3/4in) thickness in three places along, then glue and screw to main chassis 1, keeping all top edges and back ends level.

Now give it a good sanding. The main frame is now finished.
5 Cut and drill out the ends of the rear axle and mitre along both bottom edges of No. 4. Glue in a 75mm x 12mm (3in x 112in) dia dowel to take the wheels. Cut to exact length when the wheels are available. Make a packer to bridge between the two side members and under the main chassis and axle top; glue this to the top of the axle, dead centre.
6 The centre line of the rear axle is 89mm (3^1/2in) from the back end. Drill two holes in the cargo floor through to the axle; glue and screw plug holes in the cargo floor after and sand flush.
7 Shape the front axle (No. 5) and drill the steering shaft hole 25mm (1in) deep; chamfer along the bottom edge and fit the stub axles to take the wheels. You may now glue in the long steering shaft (No. 28) only, in the axle.

Box

1 For this we need Nos. 6 to 10. Drill a 51mm (2in) dia hole through No. 10 on the centre

line of the 189mm (7^5/16in) dimension, 38mm (1^1/2in) down from the top to form a rear view window. Cut out two wheel arches out of the sides, No. 9; the lower edge should coincide with No. 3.
2 Drill and counter bore to take the filling plugs at the bottom edges (three will do), and at the same time place the van front, window uppermost, between the sides keeping all top edges level and fit in between. Glue, screw and plug the sides to the side of the assembled chassis. Do not fit the roof yet.

Cab

1 Take Nos. 11 to 15 for the cab and seat. Radius the top edge of No. 14 to form the seat back; glue and tack to the front of No. 10. The cab floor (No. 13) is then glued and tacked to the chassis, also No. 12 the seat packer, then the seat which is glued on top (radius the front edge of the seat first).
2 Take the cab sides (No. 11); cut out and shape to the drawing and position these - a screw from inside No. 10 will hold these back. Keep level with the floor. Do a dry run first and trim if needed.

Engine

1 The engine block is made from Nos. 16 to 20. Glue together No. 17 face to face; when dry cut the sides with a 10° taper from a 89mm (3^1/2in) width on top. Now glue No. 16 along both sides keeping the back ends level. When dry level off the bottom edge and radius the top.
2 Shape the front (No. 19), and glue in the front of the block. Radius the front edge and top

ry

Jump aboard **Rex Coleman's** *versatile ride-on lorry and steer a course for enjoyment*

to make the bonnet shape. Glue and shape the engine block bases (No. 18) cutting out and rounding over - keep the outside edges the same width as the cargo container. Give it a good shape and sand well.

3 Cut out the dashboard (No. 20) and shape, profiling the contour of the bonnet and glue on the back of engine block, level with the floor.

Steering

1 Position the hole for the steering shaft and drill. Do not glue this engine block down; it will be secured with two screws from underneath after the collar has been fitted. Make sure the shaft turns free in the block. At this stage you must drill the cab floor (no. 13) to take the small steering column and gear lever. Angle them back about 15°- 20°.

Top: Cargo container, cab and seat, and engine block.
Above: Rear view of interior. Note the type of hinge used and the two screw holes to hold on the cab sides.
Below: The finished article showing the rear wings, front steps and wings. Note the number plate and horn press on the steering wheel.

Cutting list

Item No.	Description	Material Size Metric	Imperial	Quantity
Chassis				
1	Main chassis	38 x 168 x 622	$1^1/2$ x $6^5/8$ x $24^1/2$	1
2	Side members	19 x 54 x 433	$3/4$ x $2^1/8$ x $17^1/16$	2
3	Wheel arch strips	19 x 35 x 378	$3/4$ x $1^3/8$ x $14^7/8$	2
4	Rear axle	38 x 51 x 195	$1^1/2$ x 2 x $7^{11}/16$	1
5	Front axle	51 x 51 x 172	2 x 2 x $6^3/4$	1
Cargo container				
6	Roof	19 x 228 x 473	$3/4$ x 9 x $18^5/8$	1
7	Rear doors	19 x 89 x 175	$3/4$ x $3^1/2$ x $6^7/8$	2
8	Rear door stop	19 x 19 x 189	$3/4$ x $3/4$ x $7^5/16$	1
9	Van sides	19 x 197 x 354	$3/4$ x $7^3/4$ x $13^{15}/16$	2
10	Van front	19 x 189 x 178	$3/4$ x $7^5/16$ x 7(H)	1
Cab				
11	Cab sides	19 x 99 x 152	$3/4$ x $3^7/8$ x 6	2
12	Seat block	19 x 35 x 152	$3/4$ x $1^3/8$ x 6	1
13	Cab floor	19 x 89 x 152	$3/4$ x $3^1/2$ x 6	1
14	Seat back	10 x 101 x 152	$3/8$ x 4 x 6	1
15	Seat	10 x 41 x 152	$3/8$ x $1^5/8$ x 6	1
Engine block				
16	Block sides	19 x 73 x 146	$3/4$ x $2^7/8$ x $5^3/4$	2
17	Block top	25 x 127 x 127	1 x 5 x 5	2
18	Block base	19 x 63 x 146	$3/4$ x $2^1/2$ x $5^3/4$	2
19	Block front	19 x 89 x 190	$3/4$ x $3^1/2$ x $7^1/2$	1
20	Dashboard	10 x 78 x 190	$3/8$ x $3^1/16$ x $7^1/2$	1
Steering				
21	Bumper block front	10 x 60 x 168	$3/8$ x $2^3/8$ x $6^5/8$	1
22	Bumper block rear	10 x 57 x 222	$3/8$ x $2^1/4$ x $8^3/4$	1
23	Front bumper packer	19 x 32 x 89	$3/4$ x $1^1/4$ x $3^1/2$	1
24	Number plates	10 x 19 x 60	$3/8$ x $3/4$ x $2^3/8$	2
25	Road wheels	25 x 113 dia	1 x $4^1/2$ dia	4
26	Steering wheel (main)	25 x 230 dia	1 x 9 dia	1
27	Steering wheel hub	38 x 76 dia	$1^1/2$ x 3 dia	1
28	Steering shaft	28 x 345	$1^1/8$ dia x $13^1/2$	1
Fittings				
29	Hinges (brass; rear doors)	50	2	2 pair
30	Locking Tee Bar (brass)			1 pair
31	Furniture glides (steel)	19	$3/4$	4
32	Dowel (axles & small steering column)	457 x 13	18 x $1/2$	
33	Dowel (gear stick)	76 x 8	3 x $5/16$	
34	Wooden ball (gear knob)	16	$5/8$	1
35	Red reflectors	19	$3/4$	2
36	Dowel (axle stops)	10 x 25	$3/8$ x 1	
37	Fibre washers (wheels)	13	$1/2$	8
38	Shim between axle and chassis	29 bore	$1^1/8$ bore	1
39	Thick collar	60 o/d	$2^3/8$ o/d	1
		25 thick	1 thick	
		28 bore	$1^1/8$ bore	
40	Steering wheel (small)	64 x 13 dia	$2^1/2$ x $1/2$ dia	1

Note: For items 22 and 35, please refer to photographs. For items 26 and 27 please see figure 2.

Above: Front wheels.

2 Turn up a collar (No. 39), 60mm ($2^3/8$in) outside dia with a thickness of 25mm (1in), and bore out to suit the steering shaft. Drill and countersink to take a screw into the shaft. This holds the shaft (No. 28) in position.

3 Put a thin shim in between chassis and axle. Now lower onto the engine block. Turn the chassis over and drill through the main chassis (No. 1) into the engine block and secure with two screws. Do not glue. Does everything turn nice and easy? Good. It should now be taking shape, just a few fiddly things left to do.

Roof

1 Take the roof panel (No. 6) and run a bevel, about 25° along both sides and the back. The front edge forms the cab roof and a nice long taper of about 10°.

2 Take No. 8 and glue and tack along the back edge inside the roof to act as door stops, 40mm ($1^1/2$in) to the back edge.

3 Screw a couple of blocks inside the top and then to the side walls to hold on the roof.

Note: The rear doors (No. 7) may be hung. To hang these use 50mm flush hinges. If the

Fig. 1 Assembly of parts

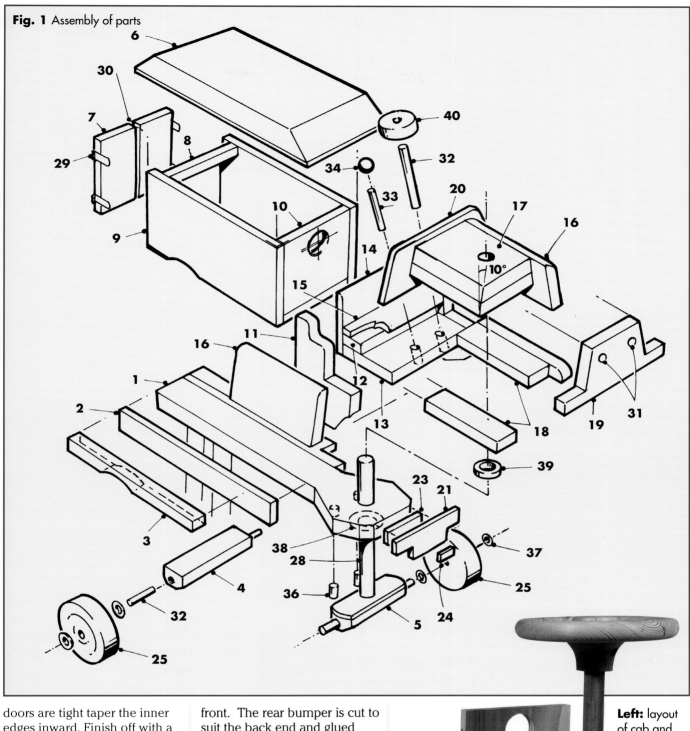

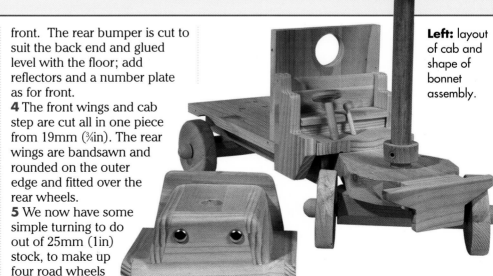

Left: layout of cab and shape of bonnet assembly.

doors are tight taper the inner edges inward. Finish off with a nice brass 'Tee' fastener.

Final assembly

1 For the front bumper (No. 21) make a packer up out of 19mm x 32mm x 89mm (^{3}/4in x 1^1/4in x 3^1/2in), glue and tack to the front of the chassis.

2 Cut out and fit to the block, making sure the wheels miss on full lock.

3 For the number plate, 10mm x 19mm x 60mm (^{3}/8in x ^{3}/4in x 2^3/8in), paint white to take 'Letraset numbers' - stick on the

front. The rear bumper is cut to suit the back end and glued level with the floor; add reflectors and a number plate as for front.

4 The front wings and cab step are cut all in one piece from 19mm (^{3}/4in). The rear wings are bandsawn and rounded on the outer edge and fitted over the rear wheels.

5 We now have some simple turning to do out of 25mm (1in) stock, to make up four road wheels

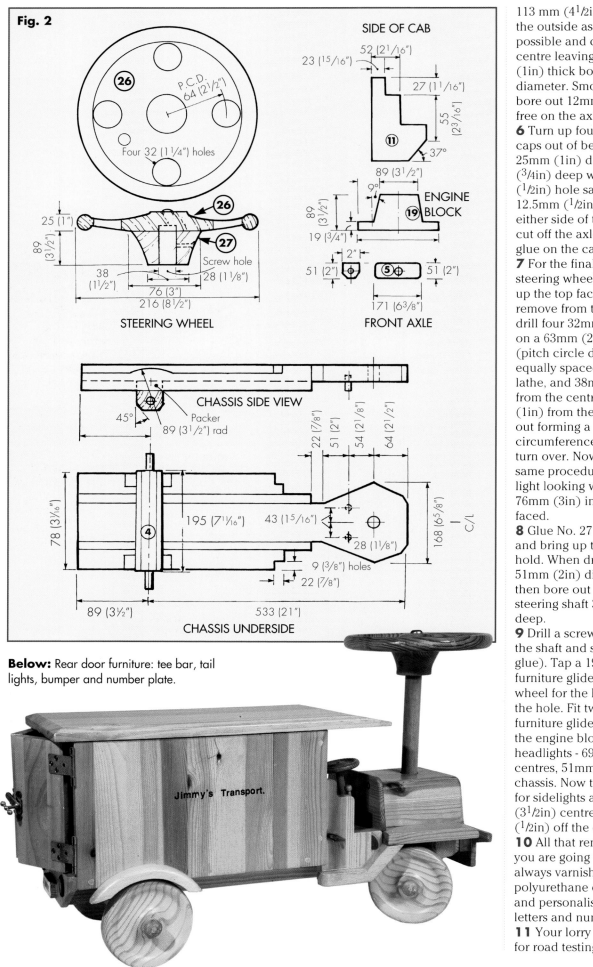

Fig. 2

P.C.D.
64 (2½")

(26)

Four 32 (1¼") holes

SIDE OF CAB

23 (¹⁵/₁₆")

52 (2¹/₁₆")

27 (1¹/₁₆")

55 (2³/₁₆")

(11)

89 (3½")

37°

ENGINE BLOCK

89 (3½")

9°

(19)

19 (¾")

2"

51 (2")

(5)

51 (2")

171 (6³/₈")

FRONT AXLE

25 (1")

89 (3½")

(26)

(27)

Screw hole

38 (1½")

28 (1⅛")

76 (3")

216 (8½")

STEERING WHEEL

CHASSIS SIDE VIEW

45°

Packer

89 (3½") rad

22 (⁷/₈")

51 (2")

54 (2¹/₈")

64 (2½")

C/L

78 (3³/₁₆")

(4)

195 (7¹¹/₁₆")

43 (1⁵/₁₆")

28 (1⅛")

168 (6⁵/₈")

9 (³/₈") holes

22 (⁷/₈")

89 (3½")

533 (21")

CHASSIS UNDERSIDE

Below: Rear door furniture: tee bar, tail lights, bumper and number plate.

Jimmy's Transport.

113 mm (4½in) dia. Leave the outside as wide as possible and dish out to the centre leaving about 25mm (1in) thick boss and same diameter. Smooth up and bore out 12mm (½in) to turn free on the axles.

6 Turn up four domed hub caps out of beech, if possible, 25mm (1in) dia x 19mm (³/4in) deep with 12.5mm (½in) hole same depth. Put 12.5mm (½in) fibre washer either side of the wheel and cut off the axle to size, then glue on the cap.

7 For the final part, the big steering wheel (No. 26), turn up the top face and rim, remove from the lathe and drill four 32mm (1¼in) holes on a 63mm (2½in) PCD (pitch circle diameter) equally spaced. Return to the lathe, and 38mm (1½in) from the centre to 25mm (1in) from the outside, dish out forming a nice round circumference; sand up and turn over. Now repeat the same procedure to get a nice light looking wheel leaving 76mm (3in) in the centre just faced.

8 Glue No. 27 to this diameter and bring up the tail stock to hold. When dry arc out to 51mm (2in) dia at the base, then bore out to suit the steering shaft 38mm (1½in) deep.

9 Drill a screw hole and fit on the shaft and secure (do not glue). Tap a 19mm (³/4in) furniture glide on top of the wheel for the horn and hide the hole. Fit two more furniture glides on the front of the engine block for headlights - 69mm (2 ³/4in) centres, 51mm (2in) off the chassis. Now two small ones for sidelights at 89mm (3½in) centres, 12.5mm (½in) off the chassis.

10 All that remains is how you are going to finish it off. I always varnish mine with polyurethane eggshell varnish and personalise with Lettraset letters and numbers.

11 Your lorry is now ready for road testing!

Riding the rails

Recapture the fun and excitement from the age of steam railways with
Victor Hatherley's *pull-along train set*

ALTHOUGH THE age of steam railways has passed, the romance and mystique lives on. The fearsome sight and sounds of the giant locos screeching and sweating to a halt at the station's edge, is an experience few of our children know. Yet strangely enough, models and toys of those unknown giants remain firm favourites of so many children to this day.

Construction
The engine
Refer to figures 1 & 2
The base of each unit in the set ('b' in figures 1 & 2) is made from 12mm (1/2in) material. I used MDF which is readily obtainable in that thickness, but solid timber may be used if preferred. The dimensions for the engine unit are 255mm x 104mm (approx 10in x 4in).

1 I prepared this first and ensured that the edges were at precise right angles to the face side. This is important throughout when fixing the truck sides to the bases.

2 Lay this aside for the moment and prepare the axle supports 'a'. Place the two together (I used a short piece of double-sided tape for the purpose) to drill the three holes for the 4mm (>3/16in) axles. It is advisable to drill these to 6mm (1/4in) allowing the wheels to

rise and fall a fraction when moving over unlevel surfaces. The positions for the three holes is shown in *figure 1*.

3 Fix the axle supports 'a' to the prepared base 'b' using PVA glue, lightly clamping until set.

4 The main boiler support 'c' is now fixed centrally on to the base *(figure 2)*. The dimensions are 175mm x 19mm x 18mm (approx 6⁷/₈in x ³/₄in x (>³/₄). This was screwed and glued to the base to ensure a durable and permanent fixing

5 The boiler component 'd' may be made in the cylindrical form as shown or if you have a lathe, an equally satisfactory one can be constructed from a square section of similar size: 45mm x 45mm (1³/₄in x 1³/₄in) section. If the cylindrical form is used, an 18mm (>³/₄in) flat should be made at the base to fit neatly on the boiler mounting 'c' as shown in *figure 2*.

6 Holes for the funnels should be drilled using the diameters suggested on *figure 1*, but approximate diameters can be used if the required drill sizes are not to hand.

7 After drilling for funnels 'f' & 'h' I continued through to the base using a smaller drill to take a No. 6 gauge screw. This enables the whole boiler to be mounted without any visible screw holes. I always add a spot of PVA on the base for extra rigidity and strength.

8 The driver's cab is straightforward. I glued and tacked the front section 'j' to the end of the boiler and the boiler mounting. Sections for the two sides 'i' are best cut together from 4mm (>³/₁₆in) MDF or ply. These too are glued and tacked to the front section 'j'. Remember to cut out the two wheel arches *(figure 1)*.

9 The roof section 'j' is shaped from solid wood and finished with 80-120 grit abrasive paper. When the adhesive is fully cured, the whole cab section should be sanded and the sharp arrises rounded over using 100 grit paper, finally sanding to a fine surface with 180-240 grit before painting. The simulated buffers and lamp are added after all the painting is completed.

The open trucks
Refer to figure 3
1 Begin in much the same way as for the engine by preparing the bases 'r'. The sizes differ of course, but the process is identical. Save time by making all three bases at the outset, i.e. two for the open trucks and one

After leaving primary school, **Victor Hatherley** *went on to study art and design in London and applied his skills in the field of display and presentation. Today, as a priest in the Church of England, Victor still finds time in his workshop to make family furniture, treen and toys.*

trucks for the moment starting with the ends 'p'. These are glued and tacked into the edges of the bases. The sides can be assembled in the same way remembering to glue the ends of 'p' to form a neat butt joint and give added strength

for the circus wagon which we will deal with later. The dimensions of each are 240mm x 90mm x 12mm (9$\frac{1}{2}$in x 3$\frac{1}{2}$in x $\frac{1}{2}$in). Again, it is important to ensure that the edges are planed square to the face side.

2 The axle supports are fixed to all three bases in the same manner as described earlier when dealing with the engine. The truck sides 'p' and 'q' in figure 3 are cut from 7mm (<$\frac{1}{4}$in) MDF or ply; 6mm ($\frac{1}{4}$in) will suit quite well if more readily available.

3 I cut all the sides for the trucks and circus wagon in one operation as they are identical. Fix only the sides of the open

The Circus Wagon
Refer to figures 4, 5 & 6

1 Having already prepared the base as suggested when making the bases for the open trucks, it remains only to drill the four holes to take the l0mm ($\frac{3}{8}$in) dowels which will form the corner supports for the roof structure *(figure 4)*. They should be drilled to approx 6mm ($\frac{1}{4}$in) depth.

2 The sides are fitted as described under the section dealing with the open trucks. It is assumed that the axle supports 's' are already in place as indicated previously. I found it best to erect the four l0mm ($\frac{3}{8}$in) dowels cutting them to length - 110mm (4$\frac{3}{8}$in); this will allow for the insertion into the base, 6mm ($\frac{1}{4}$in) and the

roof, 6mm ($\frac{1}{4}$in) as shown in *figure 4*.

3 The roof is prepared from 12mm ($\frac{1}{2}$in) MDF and is the same size exactly as the overall dimensions of truck, i.e. 260mm x 104mm (10$\frac{1}{4}$in x 3$\frac{1}{8}$in). I used the router to form the edge moulding *(figure 5)*, but if this is not available, use a plane to round over the top edge and finish with 80 grit paper wrapped around a flexible block; the silicon carbide sanding sponges supplied by Hermes are excellent for the purpose and final finishing should then be made with 120-180 grit papers.

4 The triangular capping 'v' was made from 6mm ($\frac{1}{4}$in) MDF and is housed in the centre of the roof *(figure 6)*. The decorative holes are made with spade bits held in a rigid drill stand (Forstner bits are even better if available). The sizes are not critical, but suggested diameters are 15mm (>$\frac{5}{8}$in), 10mm ($\frac{3}{8}$in) and 4mm (>$\frac{3}{16}$).

5 The completed roof canopy, 'w' and 'v', can now be glued onto the prepared dowel holes corresponding with those on the base *(figure 4)*. The circus wagon is now complete except for the addition of buffers, couplings, etc which we can add later after painting.

Painting and finishing

1 The choice of paints is a matter of personal preference, bearing in mind that lead-free paint is a must. For the undercoat/primer I always use the quick drying acrylic variety. This is available both in white and grey. The white serves as a base for the bright yellows while the grey is satisfactory under the reds and dark greens. For the bright red (engine) I found that Japlac Lacquer was excellent.

2 Use masking tape to give a clean, sharp line between contrasting colours such as parts 'v' & 'w' *(figure 5)*. When dry, the coloured bandings may now be applied to the trucks and engine. These can be obtained from motor accessory

Part	Description	Material	Dimensions	Qty
A	Axle support rail	MDF	243 x 19 x 14 (9$\frac{1}{2}$" x $\frac{3}{4}$" x $\frac{9}{16}$")	2
B	Base	MDF	255 x 104 x 12 (10" x (<4" x $\frac{1}{2}$")	1
C	Boiler mount	Soft wood	175 x 19 x 18 (6$\frac{7}{8}$" x $\frac{3}{4}$" x (>$\frac{3}{4}$")	1
D	Boiler	Soft wood	1,189 x 45 x 45 (47$\frac{5}{8}$" x 1$\frac{3}{4}$" x 1$\frac{3}{4}$")	1
E	Sides	MDF	105 x 45 x 18 (4$\frac{1}{8}$" x 1$\frac{3}{4}$" x (>$\frac{3}{4}$")	2
F	Front funnel	Beech	55 x 15 dia (2$\frac{1}{8}$" x (>$\frac{5}{8}$"),	1
G	Centre valve	Beech	12 x 20 dia ($\frac{1}{2}$" x (<$\frac{3}{4}$")	1
H	Rear valve	Beech	18 x 10 dia (>$\frac{3}{4}$" x $\frac{3}{8}$")	1
I	Driver's cab sides	MDF	135 x 63 x 4 (5$\frac{3}{8}$" x 2$\frac{1}{2}$" x (>$\frac{3}{16}$")	2
J	Driver's cab front	MDF	112 x 122 (4$\frac{3}{8}$" x 4$\frac{3}{4}$")	1
K	Screw hook	Brass	10 or 12 ($\frac{3}{8}$" or $\frac{1}{2}$")	4
L	Self-adhesive lines/bands		2 ($\frac{5}{64}$") and 4 (>$\frac{3}{16}$"), 1 of each roll	2
M	Lettraset rub-on letters & numerals			1
N	Decadry logo (rub-on designs)			2
O	Hub caps		To fit 6 ($\frac{1}{4}$") axle	18
P	Truck ends	MDF	90 x 36 x 7 (3$\frac{1}{2}$" x 1$\frac{3}{8}$" x (<$\frac{1}{4}$")	6
Q	Truck sides	MDF	260 x 36 x 7 (10$\frac{1}{4}$" x 1$\frac{3}{8}$" x $\frac{1}{2}$")	6
R	Truck bases	MDF	240 x 90 x 12 (9$\frac{1}{2}$" x 3$\frac{1}{2}$" x $\frac{1}{2}$")	3
S	Axle support rails	MDF	240 x 20 x 14 (9$\frac{1}{2}$" x <$\frac{3}{4}$" x $\frac{9}{16}$")	6
T	Screw eyes	Brass	10 or 12 ($\frac{3}{8}$" x $\frac{1}{2}$")	3
U	Dowels/roof supports		110 x 10 dia (4$\frac{3}{8}$" x $\frac{3}{8}$")	4
V	Roof, centre apex capping		228 x 16 x 6 (9' x $\frac{5}{8}$" x $\frac{1}{4}$")	1
W	Roof of circus wagon	MDF	260 x 104 x 12 (10$\frac{1}{4}$" x 4" x $\frac{1}{2}$")	1
X	Wheels		50 (2") dia	18
Y	Axle	Steel	6 ($\frac{1}{4}$") dia x 850 approx	1
Z	Washers	Thin steel	6 ($\frac{1}{4}$") centre	18

Cutting list (metric measurements first)

stockists or model shops.

3 To simulate the buffer stops, I used polished brass upholstery studs. To ensure safety, I added a spot of Araldite adhesive to the inside of the head before tacking each into place.

4 Couplings were made from brass screw-threaded hooks and eyes. Choose those with the longest screw thread for greater strength and security. These are obtainable in various types and sizes from most DIY stockists.

5 The lettering, numerals and logos were all applied from sheets of rub-on lettering, such as that of Lettraset or similar brands. These are available from all good stationers and artists' materials suppliers.

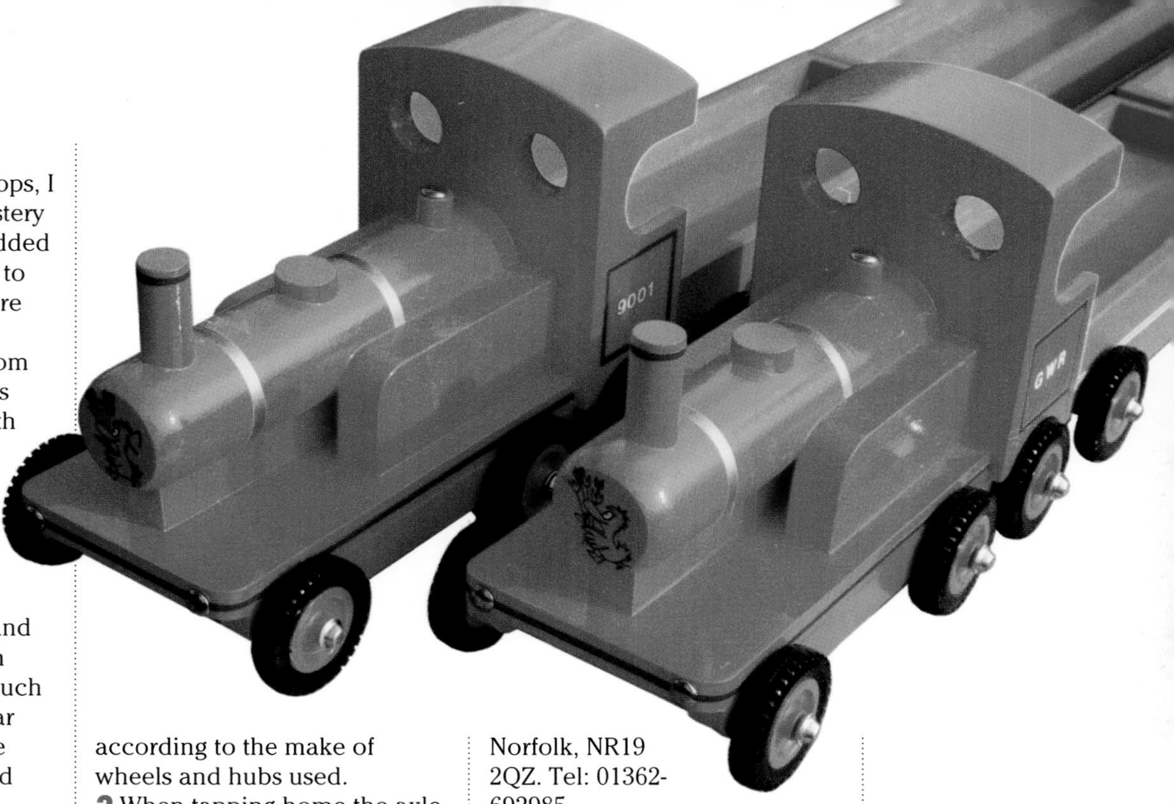

Mounting the wheels

1 When cutting the axles to length, remember to add to the overall width of the engine/truck, the thickness of the wheel hubs x 2 and the depth of the axles caps x 2, plus 2mm (5/64in) for clearance and two washers. These measurements will vary according to the make of wheels and hubs used.

2 When tapping home the axle caps, I usually add a small amount of Loctite's 'Lock'n Seal' to the inside of the hub cap as this adds further strength.

Suppliers

Wheels, axles, hub caps, etc available from:

● Hobbies (Dereham) Ltd, 34-36 Swaffham Road, Dereham, Norfolk, NR19 2QZ. Tel: 01362-692985.

● Hobby's, Knight's Hill Square, London, SE27 OHH. Tel: 0181-761-4244

● K-Toys, Unit 1, Second Avenue, Westfield Trading Estate, Midsomer Norton, Bath BA3 4BH. Tel: 01761-411299.

● Craft Supplies, The Mill, Millers Dale, Nr Buxton, Derbyshire, SK17 8SN. Freephone 0800-146417.

Fig. 1 Side elevation of engine.
Wheels used are 50 (2") dia, mounted on 4mm axles (>3/16")

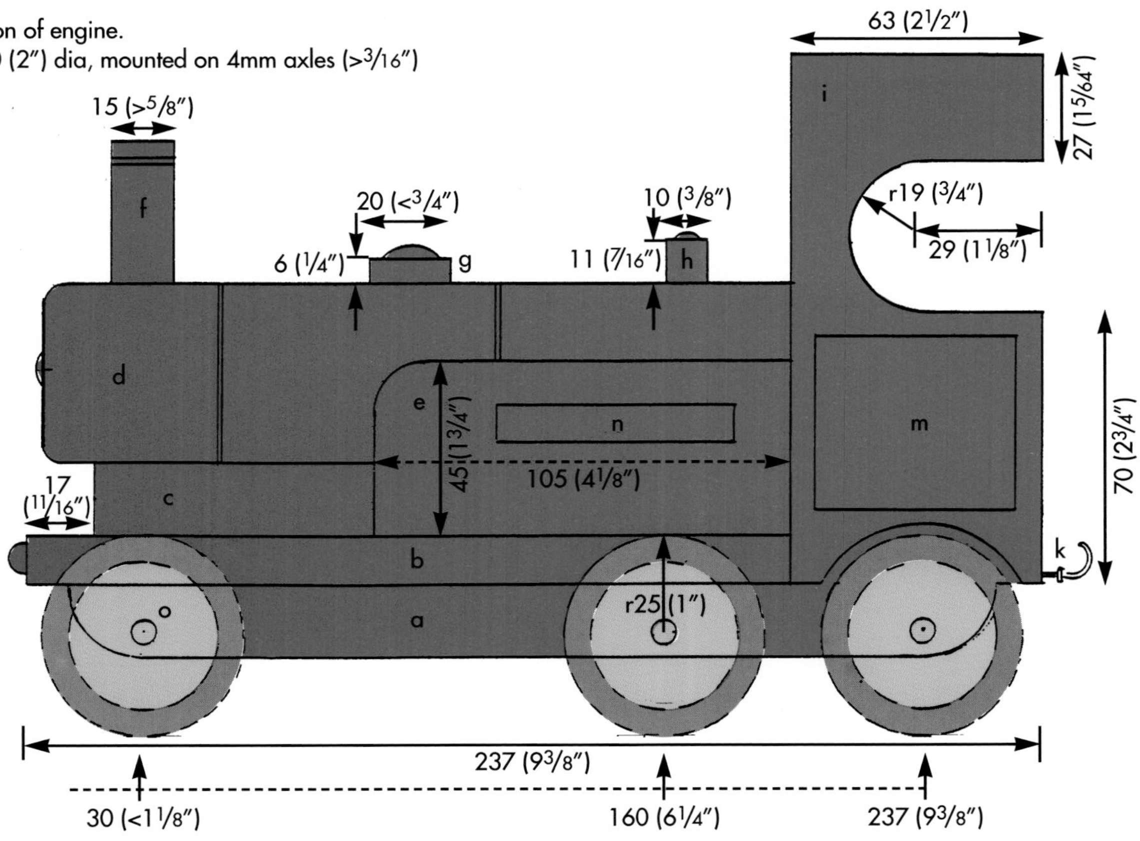

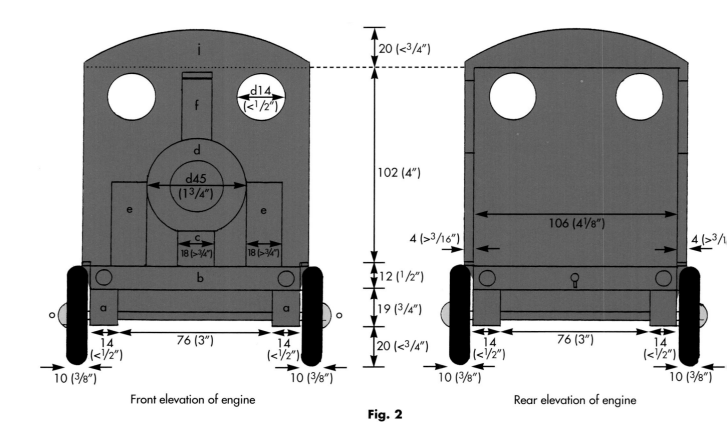

Front elevation of engine

Fig. 2

Rear elevation of engine

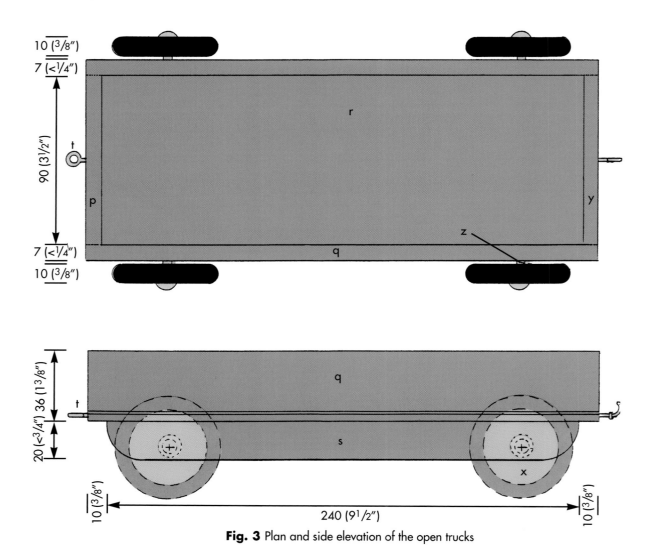

Fig. 3 Plan and side elevation of the open trucks

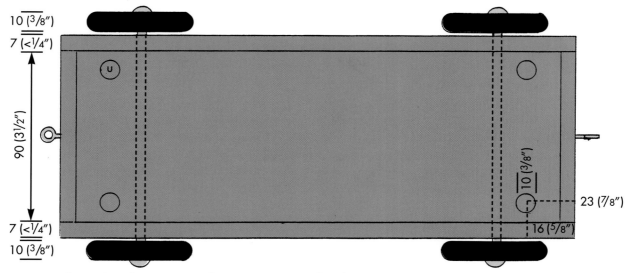

Fig. 4 Plan of circus wagon showing positioning of roof supports (plan of roof canopy not shown)

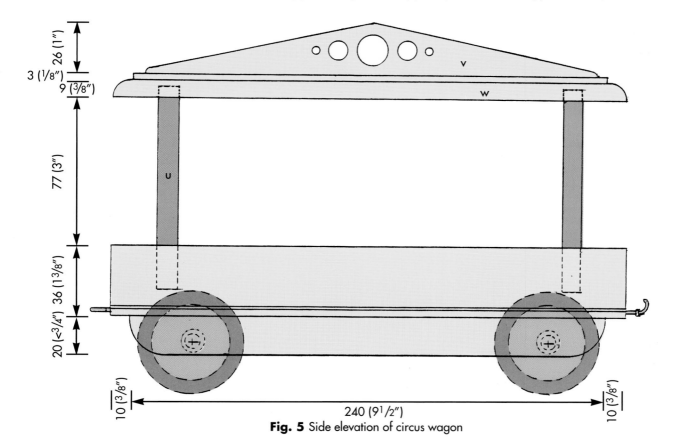

Fig. 5 Side elevation of circus wagon

Fig. 6 Circus wagon. Detail of canopy plan showing position of the central ridge decorative feature. The moulded edges were made with 10 (³⁄₈") rad router bit. The ridge is housed in 6 (¹⁄₄") recess approx 4 (>³⁄₁₆") in depth.

HMS NEPTU

These fighting ships by Ivor Carlyle will captivate young salts

"Uncle Ivor, can we play with the ships that fire cannon balls again?"

A toy that is not only remembered but sought after proves what a success this design is.

Details for two designs are covered, H.M.S. Neptune and the pirate ship 'Scallywag', both of which are pushed along on wheels. There is a space on board for a captain and four crew, but the most exciting features are the working cannons which fire table tennis balls when the firing pins are hit with the firing hammer. Best results are obtained from the cheap 38mm 'ping pong' balls sold as toys. Quality table tennis balls are more energy absorbing and don't work as well.

The construction and materials required for H.M.S. Neptune and the pirate ship 'Scallywag' are identical. The only things that need to be different are the crew members, flag and sail patterns and the figurehead and nameplates. All these details are shown on the plans and can be seen also on the photographs. Of course, you may prefer to make up your own names and paint finishes for the completed ships.

Tools

A fretsaw and drill in a vertical drill-stand are the most important tools required; the rest, such as a small block plane or Surform, make up the average DIY toolkit. I would like to put in a word here for the DAVID balsa plane. Designed for modelling balsa wood and using disposable blades, it also works superbly well on pine, ply, MDF and wherever you need to finely shave wood. A further bonus is that it's cheap.

RULES OF ENGAGEMENT

The thing about pirates is they don't fight by rules but my nephews have come up with the following. Manoeuvre your ship into position and hit your opponent's ship with a broadside before they hit yours.

The winner then lines up the opponent's crew and sees how many they can knock down with a broadside. This then becomes their score before starting again. At the end of play the scores are added up to decide the winner.

and scallywag

NE

Construction

❶ Begin by cutting out two pieces of 12.5mm pine slightly longer than the base, and butt joint them together to form one wide plank. Clamping them in a Workmate is ideal. Cut to shape the base, keel, sides, transom, aft deck and the bow sides. Drill all the holes required in the base and keel before joining together, and then check for squareness of fit. Add the quadrant along the length of the keel where it meets the base. Pin and glue the sides onto the base followed by the transom. Make a bevel on the rear edge of the aft deck to match the slope of the transom, then fit into position. Glue together the pine bow sections in the following way: one section of A, four sections of B and then another of A.

Bow/top keel

❶ Tape or pin into position bow/top keel (this is the piece that holds the bowsprit and figurehead) but do not glue. Offer up the bow sections and check and adjust for fit. Before gluing, smooth up the inner surface with glasspaper wrapped around a small can or other suitable shape. Glue into their final position but avoid gluing to the bow/top keel, which must be removed to allow shaping of the bow section. While using clamps and masking tape to hold everything in place until set, remove the bow/top keel.

❷ Fit the side rails to the inside edge as shown on Fig 1 and Fig 4. Shape the bow with either a plane, Surform or David plane. The ideal way to hold the hull while doing this is to clamp it carefully in a Workmate.

❸ Avoid taking too much off in one go and check frequently for

Materials

- 12.5mm (½in) Prepared pine or equivalent softwood in plank width of 90mm (3½in) minimum
- 6mm (¼in) Plywood – Birch multiply is best for toys
- 6mm (¼in) and 12.5mm (½in) Hardwood dowel
- 9mm (⅜in) Quadrant
- Small amount of coarse linen for sail and flag
- Plain postcards for cannon barrels
- Eight No 6 x ½in Parallel shank chipboard type screws
- ½in Brass fret pins
- Two ½in x 1¼in –1½in Compression springs
- Eight ¼in washers
- A short length of braided nylon cord
- One Pipe cleaner
- PVA woodworking adhesive and epoxy resin adhesive
- Waterproof coloured felt tips or inks
- Non toxic coloured enamel/ lacquer paints and transparent varnish (ie Japlac, Humbrol)
- One 37mm (1½in) Hardwood ball

PLEASE NOTE: the author supplied drawings with metric measurements, and we recommend you use those. The imperial sizes given are the nearest equivalent.

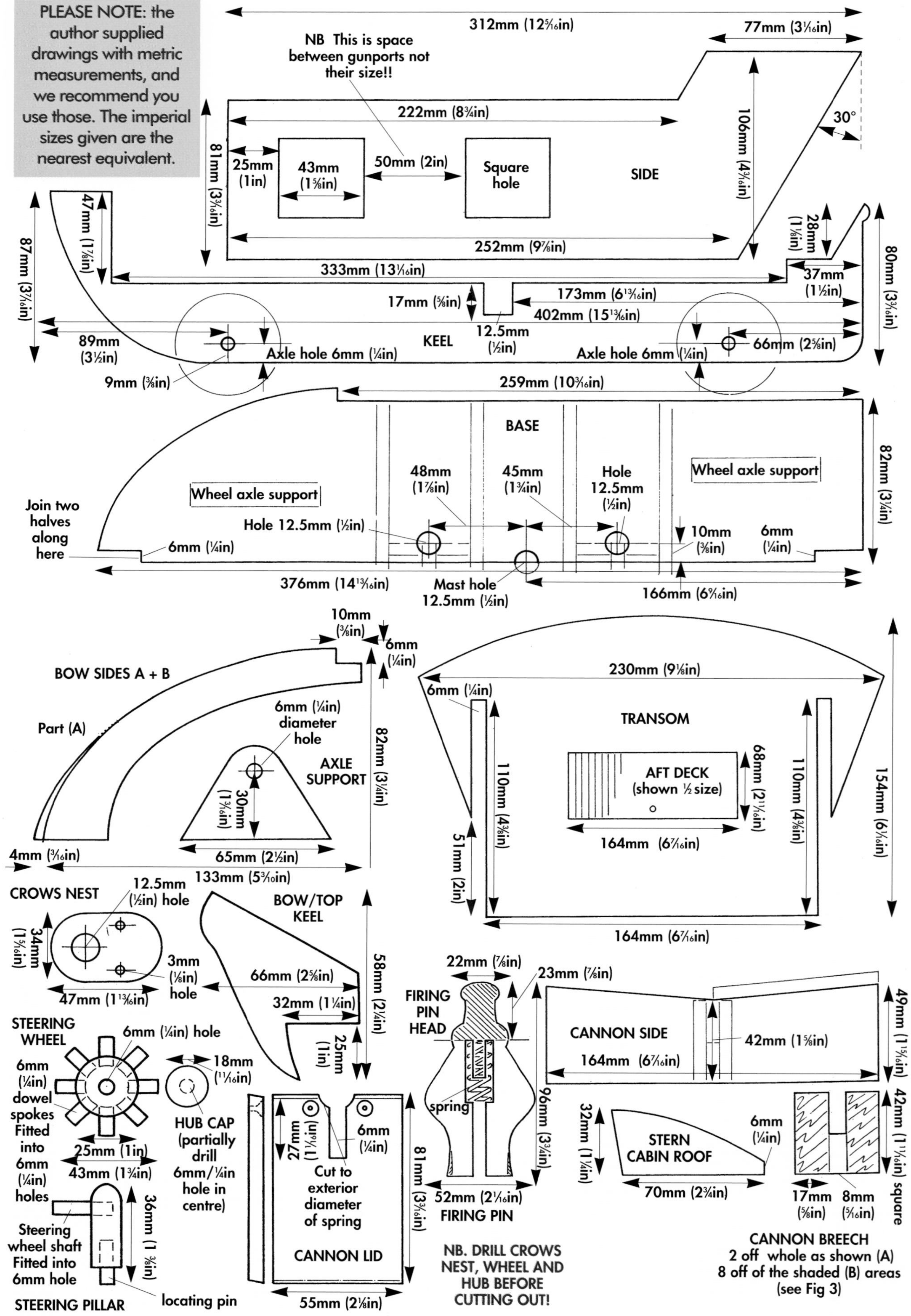
312mm (12 5/16in)
77mm (3 1/16in)
NB This is space between gunports not their size!!
222mm (8 3/4in)
30°
106mm (4 3/16in)
81mm (3 3/16in)
25mm (1in)
43mm (1 5/8in)
50mm (2in)
Square hole
SIDE
252mm (9 7/8in)
28mm (1 1/8in)
87mm (3 7/16in)
47mm (1 7/8in)
333mm (13 1/16in)
37mm (1 1/2in)
80mm (3 3/16in)
17mm (5/8in)
173mm (6 13/16in)
402mm (15 13/16in)
89mm (3 1/2in)
KEEL
12.5mm (1/2in)
66mm (2 5/8in)
Axle hole 6mm (1/4in)
Axle hole 6mm (1/4in)
9mm (3/8in)
259mm (10 3/16in)
BASE
82mm (3 1/4in)
48mm (1 7/8in)
45mm (1 3/4in)
Hole 12.5mm (1/2in)
Wheel axle support
Wheel axle support
Join two halves along here
Hole 12.5mm (1/2in)
6mm (1/4in)
10mm (3/8in)
6mm (1/4in)
376mm (14 13/16in)
Mast hole 12.5mm (1/2in)
166mm (6 9/16in)
10mm (3/8in)
6mm (1/4in)
BOW SIDES A + B
Part (A)
6mm (1/4in) diameter hole
AXLE SUPPORT
30mm (1 3/16in)
82mm (3 1/4in)
4mm (3/16in)
65mm (2 1/2in)
133mm (5 3/10in)
230mm (9 1/8in)
6mm (1/4in)
TRANSOM
AFT DECK (shown 1/2 size)
68mm (2 11/16in)
110mm (4 3/8in)
110mm (4 3/8in)
154mm (6 1/16in)
164mm (6 7/16in)
51mm (2in)
164mm (6 7/16in)
CROWS NEST
12.5mm (1/2in) hole
34mm (1 5/16in)
3mm (1/8in) hole
47mm (1 13/16in)
BOW/TOP KEEL
66mm (2 5/8in)
32mm (1 1/4in)
58mm (2 1/4in)
25mm (1in)
STEERING WHEEL
6mm (1/4in) hole
6mm (1/4in) dowel spokes Fitted into 6mm (1/4in) holes
18mm (11/16in)
HUB CAP (partially drill 6mm/1/4in hole in centre)
25mm (1in)
43mm (1 3/4in)
36mm (1 3/8in)
Steering wheel shaft Fitted into 6mm hole
STEERING PILLAR
locating pin
27mm (1 1/16in)
6mm (1/4in)
Cut to exterior diameter of spring
81mm (3 3/16in)
CANNON LID
55mm (2 1/8in)
22mm (7/8in)
23mm (7/8in)
FIRING PIN HEAD
spring
96mm (3 3/4in)
52mm (2 1/16in)
FIRING PIN
NB. DRILL CROWS NEST, WHEEL AND HUB BEFORE CUTTING OUT!
CANNON SIDE
164mm (6 7/16in)
42mm (1 5/8in)
49mm (1 15/16in)
32mm (1 1/4in)
STERN CABIN ROOF
6mm (1/4in)
70mm (2 3/4in)
42mm (1 11/16in) square
17mm (5/8in)
8mm (5/16in)
CANNON BREECH
2 off whole as shown (A)
8 off of the shaded (B) areas
(see Fig 3)

Cutting list	
Pine – 12.5mm (1/2in)	
1 x Base	376 x 164mm (14 13/16 x 6 1/2in)
1 x Keel	402 x 87mm (15 13/16 x 3 7/16in)
8 x Bow sides (B)	82 x 137mm (3 1/4 x 5 3/8in)
4 x Bow sides (A)	82 x 133mm (3 1/4 x 5 3/16in)
1 x Bow/Top keel	66 x 83mm (2 5/8in x 3 1/4in)
4 x Axle supports	65 x 40mm (2 1/2 x 1 9/16in)
4 x Wheels	53mm (2 1/8in) diameter
1 x Steering wheel hub	25mm (1in) diameter
1 x Bowsprit collar	25mm (1in) diameter
1 x Flagpole cap	19mm (3/4in) diameter
2 x Flagpole supports	19mm (3/4in) diameter
1 x Mast cap	38mm (1 1/2in) diameter
1 x Crows nest	47 x 34mm (1 13/16 x 1 5/16in)
10 x Arms	36 x 30mm (1 7/16 x 1 3/16in)
1 x Captain (double thickness)	103 x 49mm (4 x 1 15/16in)
1 x Crew (double thickness)	103 x 38mm (4 x 1 1/2in)
Plywood – 6mm (1/4in)	
2 x Sides	312 x 106mm (12 5/16 x 4 3/16in)
1 x Transom	230 x 154mm (9 1/8 x 6 1/16in)
1 x Aft deck	164 x 68mm (6 7/16 x 2 11/16in)
2 x Stern cabin roofs	70 x 32mm (2 3/4in x 1 1/4in)
2 x Side rails	222 x 6mm (8 3/4 x 1/4in)
4 x Gunport doors	56 x 56mm (2 1/4 x 2 1/4in)
4 x Cannon sides	164 x 49mm (6 7/16 x 1 15/16in)
2 x Cannon breeches (A)	42 x 42mm (1 11/16 x 1 11/16in)
8 x Cannon breeches (B)	17 x 42mm (11/16 x 1 11/16in)
4 x Cannon lids	81 x 55mm (3 3/16 x 2 1/8in)
4 x Wheel hub caps	18mm (11/16in) diameter
1 x Steering wheel hub cap	18mm (11/16in) diameter
1 x Figurehead	64mm (2 1/2in) diameter
3 x Nameplates	64 x 16mm (2 1/2 x 5/8in)
4 x Large hat discs	44mm (1 3/4in) diameter (Neptune only)
4 x Small hat discs	28mm (1 1/8in) diameter (Neptune only)
2 x Firing pins	96 x 52mm (3 3/4 x 2in)
4 x Firing pin tops	23 x 22mm (7/8 x 7/8in)
Dowel – 12.5mm (1/4in)	
1 x Steering pillar	36mm (1 3/8in)
1 x Bowsprit	117mm (4 5/8in)
1 x Mast	335mm (13 1/4in)
1 x Hammer shaft	175mm (6 7/8in)
Dowel – 6mm (1/4in)	
2 x Axles	118mm (4 5/8in)
1 x Steering locating pin	20mm (13/16in)
1 x Steering wheel shaft	25mm (1in)
8 x Spokes	14mm (9/16in)
1 x Bowsprit locating pin	20mm (13/16in)
1 x Flagpole	148mm (5 13/16in)
1 x Spar	152mm (6in)
Quadrant – 9mm (3/8in)	
2 x Keel fillets	376mm (14 13/16in)
1 x Wood ball	37mm (1 1/2in) diameter
4 x Barrel liners (postcard)	141 x 64mm (5 1/2 x 2 1/2in)
1 x Sail (linen)	215 x 180mm (8 1/2 x 7 1/8in)
1 x Flag (linen)	155 x 75mm (6 1/8 x 3in)

symmetry and smoothness of shape. When you think you've almost reached the final shape, start to use a medium grade glasspaper. Follow with a fine grade to smooth out and blend in the various parts.

❹ Glue the gunport doors to the ships' sides. The 43mm round hole in the door must line up with the 43mm square hole in the sides as shown on Fig 4.

❺ Next glue the axle supports into position, as indicated on the plan view of the base. Fig 4 shows the front wheel assembly completed. Temporarily insert the axle dowels to ensure accurate alignment. Glue into position the bow/top keel and also the stern cabin roofs.

Breech assembly

❶ Assemble the cannon breech components A and B as shown in Fig 3 by gluing two parts B to each side of part A. The firing pins are made by cutting out the entire shape shown on the plan. The part shown by the shading is then glued to each side of the firing pin head as shown on Fig 5.

❷ Before fitting the breech assembly into position check that the firing pin rides freely up and down in the breech slots and in and out of the holes in the base. Fig 4 shows the firing pin in its up position.

Cannon sides

❶ Glue the cannon sides into position on the base between the square holes in the sides. Fig 1 shows one of the sides in position. Now fit the breech assembly into position as shown in Fig 2 and Fig 4.

❷ Check again that the firing pins move freely up and down, sanding down surface and edges on the firing pin if necessary. Rubbing candle wax onto the moving parts will greatly enhance freedom of movement.

Cannon lids

❶ Place the cannon lids into position and drill 2mm pilot holes into the breech for the screws. Fit the firing pin with its spring into position as shown in Fig 4 and place the lids on top as shown in Fig 2. A little jiggling about may be needed to get the lids into position before finally fitting the screws.

❷ Cut the cannon barrel liners out of postcard, roll into a tube and glue

Fig 1
Main hull assembly

Note mast, firing pin, axles and steering post holes

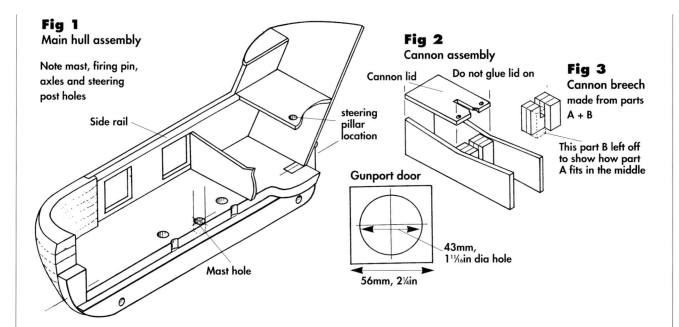

Side rail

steering pillar location

Mast hole

Fig 2
Cannon assembly

Cannon lid

Do not glue lid on

Fig 3
Cannon breech
made from parts A + B

This part B left off to show how part A fits in the middle

Gunport door

43mm, 1¹¹⁄₁₆in dia hole

56mm, 2¼in

---

along area shown. Fit into gunport, gluing the end nearest to the firing pin onto the base. See Fig 4.

❸ The idea is, as the barrel liners and any of the other parts wear, the lids can be unscrewed and serviced. To check the firing action, load the balls and strike the firing pin with the hammer. It's not purely force but a quick sharp action that flicks the balls out.

❹ Dismantle the cannons before painting.

❺ Varnish all surfaces apart from the interior of the cannons. Use decorators' tape to divide the colours along the sides when painting. Slide the crow's nest onto the mast.

Mast

❶ The mast is fitted by inserting its end into the mast hole shown on the plan and on Fig 1. Do not glue into place; ensure it is a tight fit but can be removed for stowage and repair work.

❷ Assembly of the bowsprit and flagpole are shown on Figs 6 and 7. Counter bore the back of the figurehead to take a 12mm length of 6mm dowel: this is used to locate it in a hole on the bowsprit. The bowsprit assembly, nameplates, and flagpole parts are glued on with epoxy resin adhesive after scraping the contact surfaces with a knife.

❸ Fit 6mm dowel axles through the axle supports and keel. Place a

Figs 6 and 7
Bowsprit and flagpole assembly

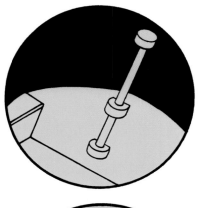

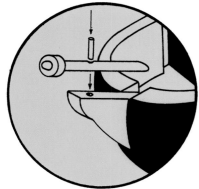

washer each side of the wheels before gluing with epoxy resin the counter bored hubs onto the ends.

Steering wheel

❶ Fit the eight spokes into the steering wheel and place it onto the steering wheel shaft followed by the hub cap. The locating pin at the base of the steering pillar is glued into the locating hole shown on Fig 1.

Fig 4

Gunport door

Side rail

Breech

Firing pin

Firing pin

Cannon lid

Cannon barrel liner

Ping pong ball

Firing pin holes

Fig 5

❷ The windows can be photocopied, coloured in with waterproof coloured inks, then glued onto the ship with PVA glue, after being slightly dampened. When thoroughly dry, varnish over.

Sail

❶ Wrap the top of the sail around the spar with PVA glue and drill a 2mm hole in each end to take the cord which suspends it from the crow's nest.
❷ Fold up the sail bottom to encapsulate a pipe cleaner. Seams and other detail can be put on with a pen.
❸ Cut the crew from pieces of 12.5mm pine, glued together to form 25mm thick portions. Cut the arms from single thickness pine and glue onto the sides of the body.

Once the crew is aboard you will be ready to sail. Bon voyage! ●

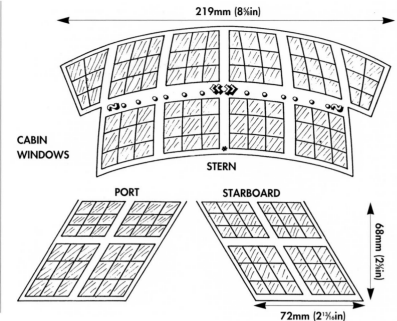

CABIN WINDOWS

219mm (8⅝in)

STERN

PORT   STARBOARD

68mm (2⅝in)

72mm (2¹³⁄₁₆in)

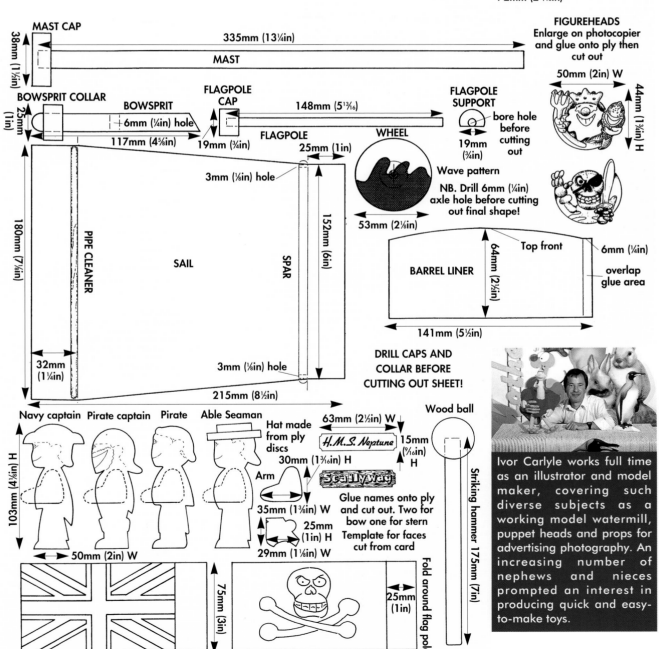

MAST CAP

38mm (1½in)

MAST

335mm (13¼in)

FIGUREHEADS
Enlarge on photocopier and glue onto ply then cut out

50mm (2in) W

44mm (1¾in) H

BOWSPRIT COLLAR

25mm (1in)

BOWSPRIT

6mm (¼in) hole

117mm (4⅝in)

FLAGPOLE CAP

19mm (¾in)

FLAGPOLE

148mm (5¹³⁄₁₆)

25mm (1in)

WHEEL

Wave pattern

53mm (2⅛in)

NB. Drill 6mm (¼in) axle hole before cutting out final shape!

FLAGPOLE SUPPORT

bore hole before cutting out

19mm (¾in)

3mm (⅛in) hole

152mm (6in)

PIPE CLEANER

180mm (7⅛in)

SAIL

SPAR

32mm (1¼in)

3mm (⅛in) hole

215mm (8½in)

BARREL LINER

Top front

64mm (2½in)

6mm (¼in)

overlap glue area

141mm (5½in)

DRILL CAPS AND COLLAR BEFORE CUTTING OUT SHEET!

Navy captain   Pirate captain   Pirate   Able Seaman

103mm (4¹/₁₆in) H

50mm (2in) W

Hat made from ply discs

30mm (1³⁄₁₆in) H

Arm

35mm (1⅜in) W

25mm (1in) H

29mm (1⅛in) W

63mm (2½in) W

H.M.S. Neptune   15mm (⁹⁄₁₆in) H

Scallywag

Glue names onto ply and cut out. Two for bow one for stern
Template for faces cut from card

Wood ball

Striking hammer 175mm (7in)

75mm (3in)

25mm (1in)

Fold around flag pole

155mm (6in)

Stiffen flags with emulsion or white paint before colouring in

Ivor Carlyle works full time as an illustrator and model maker, covering such diverse subjects as a working model watermill, puppet heads and props for advertising photography. An increasing number of nephews and nieces prompted an interest in producing quick and easy-to-make toys.

The game is afoot!

Find the winning solutions to Diamond Solitaire and Chinese Towers. Great fun for the whole family. David Mackenzie explains the rules

Both games are made with moveable pieces held firmly in place on the board.

I was shown Diamond Solitaire by a friend who had learned about it from his grandfather. He was not sure whether it was a game for two people or a puzzle for one. It took several weeks to work out that it was a puzzle and how to solve it. The solution is not very easy and left to my own devices I might still be working on it, but fortunately I had help from another friend who is a puzzle expert. I have included her solution (*figure 1*).

Chinese Towers is a game for two players that was described to me by yet another friend who was introduced to it during a cruise around the Norwegian fjords.

For both games the wood used is not important, but I chose oak because I wanted to make them look as attractive as possible; the intention was to present them to the friends who had brought them to my attention in the first place.

Diamond Solitaire

In the labelled board the letters refer to the holes in the board and not the pegs. So if the instructions say 'c–X' it means the contents of the hole 'c' move to hole 'X', and the colour of the peg is irrelevant.

c–X. G–c, I–G, X–I, B–X, h–B, i–h, X–i, a–X, d–a, i–d, g–i, c–g, G–c, X–G, A–X, F–A, I–F, H–I, B–H, h–B, i–h, X–i, A–X, C–A, G–c, E–G, B–E, h–B, e–h, c–e, X–c, a–X, c–a, G–c, I–G, X–I, h–X, b–h, a–b, c–a, G–c, X–G, A–X, B–A, h–B, X–h

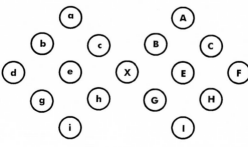

Fig. 1

Diamond Solitaire

The object of this game – played by one person – is to get all of the blue pegs up to the white peg end of the board and *vice versa*. The pegs move one place at a time and must never move backwards, but they can jump over pegs of either colour.

Diamond Solitaire
Cutting List (All sizes are actual)

No.	Description	Material	Size (mm)	Size (inches)
1 off	Playing board	Oak	127 x 76 x 9	5 x 3 x 3/8
1 off	Box end	Oak	89 x 18 x 6	3½ x ¾ x ¼
1 off	Box end	Oak	89 x 25 x 6	3½ x 1 x ¼
1 off	Box sides	Oak	140 x 25 x 6	5½ x 1 x ¼
1 off	Box lid	Oak	140 x 83 x 6	5½ x 3 ¼ x ¼
1 off	Pegs	Ramin	144 mm long x 9mm dia.	9/16 long x 3/8 dia.

Game board

1 Cut the board to size and mark out the grid with a pencil as shown in *figure 2*. Where the lines intersect make a hole with a bradawl to act as a drill guide. Then, with an electric drill mounted in a drill stand so that the holes are vertical, drill a pilot hole with a 3mm (1/8in) drill bit to a depth of 8mm (5/16in). This is followed by drilling the holes to a diameter of 9mm (3/8in) which is the final size. The edges of the holes are chamfered with a large countersink bit.

2 Using a black felt tipped pen and a ruler draw the connecting lines between the holes to indicate the direction in which the pegs can move.

Fig.2 Layout of the board Each square = 12mm (½in)

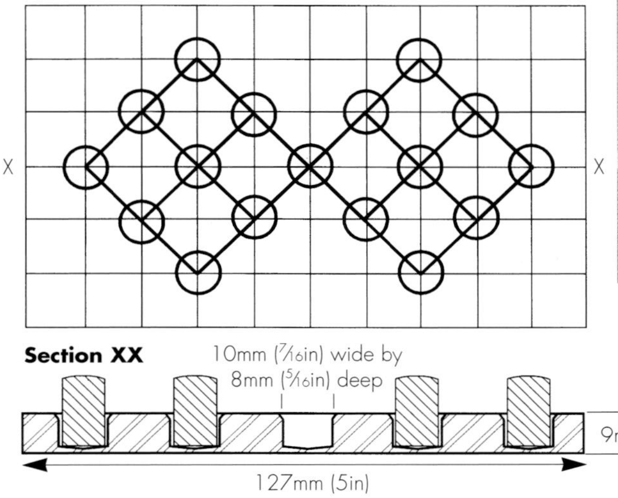

X
X
Section XX
10mm (7/16in) wide by
8mm (5/16in) deep
9mm (3/8in)
127mm (5in)

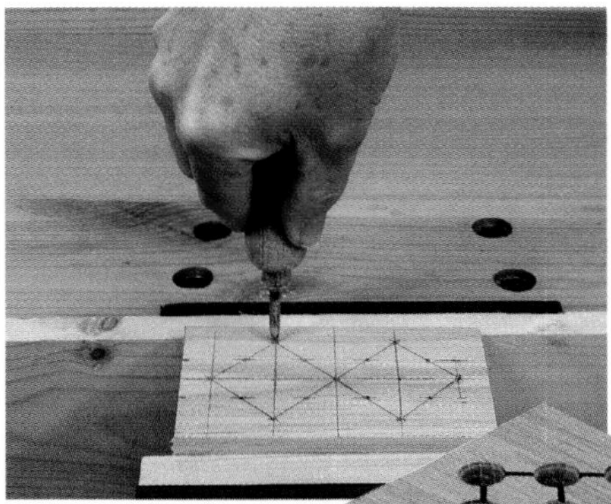

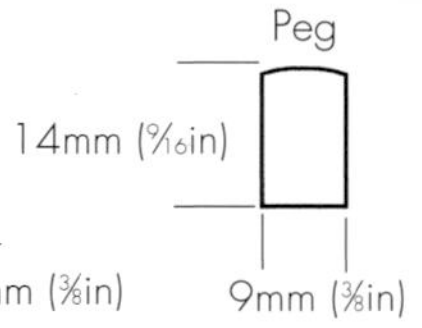

Peg
14mm (9/16in)
9mm (3/8in)

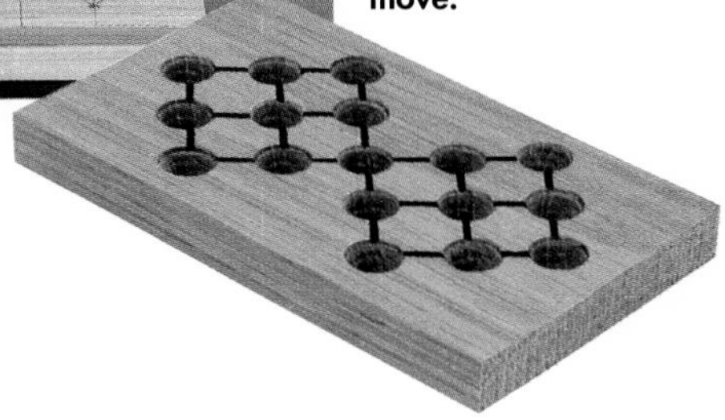

Left **Where the lines intersect make a hole with a bradawl to act as a drill guide.**
Below **Draw connecting lines between the holes to indicate the direction in which the pegs can move.**

Box

1 Refer to *figures 3 and 4*. To make the two long sides, cut pieces of oak to the size shown in the drawing and make a groove in them where the lid will eventually slide; use a router with a 3mm (1/8in) cutter. When making the joints on the ends use dividers to mark the width of the pins for the box joint and a try-square to mark their length. After doing this on all four ends, cut down the sides of

Fig.3

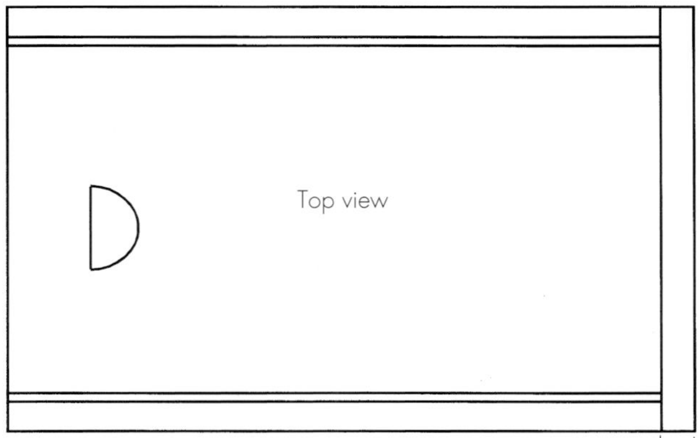

Top view

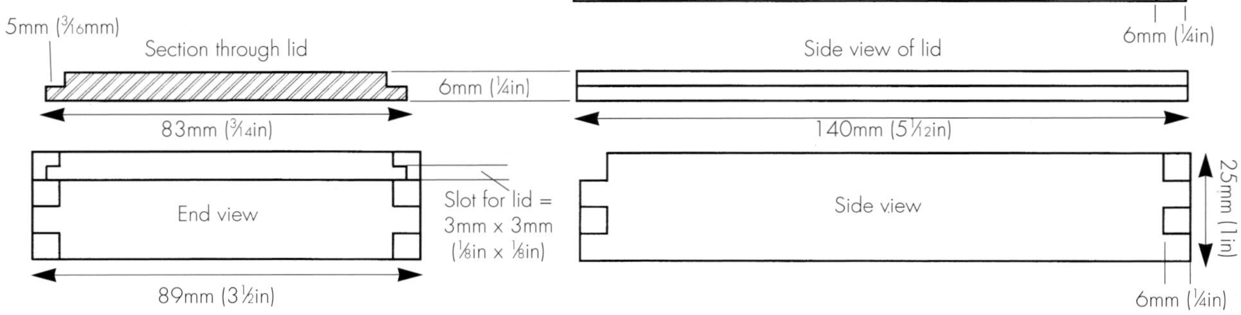

5mm (3/16mm)
Section through lid
6mm (¼in)
83mm (3¼in)
Side view of lid
6mm (¼in)
140mm (5½in)
End view
Slot for lid = 3mm x 3mm (1/8in x 1/8in)
89mm (3½in)
Side view
25mm (1in)
6mm (¼in)

Fig.4

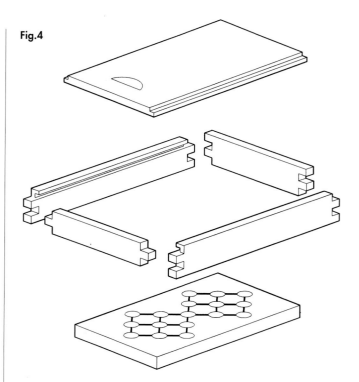

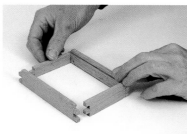

Above **Use a bevel-edged chisel to par up to the line.**
Left **The joints are assembled dry to test for accuracy.**

the pins in the waste wood area with a tenon saw. Remove most of the waste wood with a coping saw and then use a bevel-edged chisel to par up to the line.

② The two short sides are cut to size and the box joints are marked out using the joints already made on the long sides as a template. Indicate the waste wood areas by cross hatching with a pencil and form the joint as before.

③ The joints on all four sides are assembled dry to test for accuracy and adjusted if required. They are then glued and clamped.

④ When the sides are secure, glue is placed around the edge of the games board and it is fitted into the assembled sides. When this is secure the joints are cleaned up with a plane and glasspaper.

⑤ A piece of oak is prepared to the correct size for the lid and rebated on the edges so that it slides in the grooves made in the sides with a rebating plane. In order to open the box lid a notch is cut in the top of the lid so that it can be pushed open with a thumb nail. A marking knife and a 12mm (½in) gouge are used for this.

A marking knife and a 12mm (½in) gouge is used to make a notch in the top of the lid.

④ The pegs are cut from 9mm (⅜in) dowel, and the ends are smoothed and slightly rounded with glasspaper.

The pegs are cut from 9mm (⅜in) dowel.

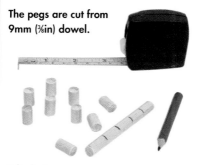

Finish

All parts are made smoother with progressively finer grades of glass-paper, until a satisfactory surface finish is achieved. This is followed with two applications of 'golden oak' brushing wax. It is applied and allowed to dry before buffing it off with a soft cloth. The pegs are clear varnished and the top end is painted in bright colours with enamel paint.

The pegs are clear varnished and the top end is painted in bright colours with enamel paint.

Chinese Towers

The beads are divided between two players, one set of colours for each. Starting with an empty board each person places a bead on a peg in any position on the board. The winner is decided when one of the players manages to lay four beads in a straight line in any direction. The opposing player tries to prevent this from happening by blocking the other player with his/her beads while trying to lay a continuous row of four beads himself. A winning row of beads can be in any direction: vertical, horizontal or diagonal.

A winning row in Chinese Towers can be in any direction: vertical, horizontal or diagonal.

Fig.5

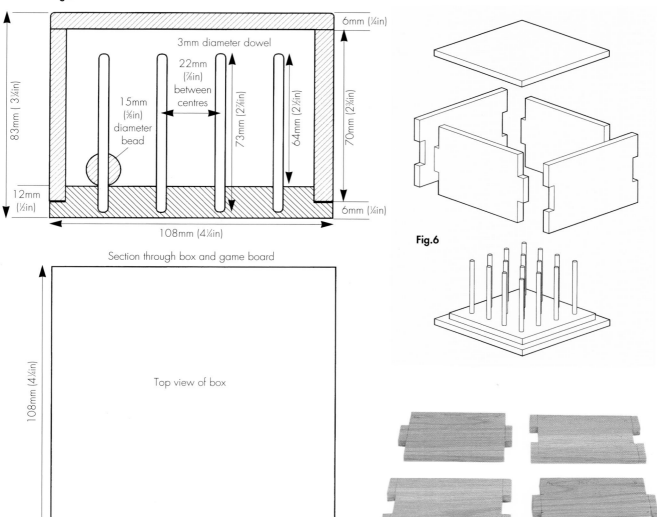

Section through box and game board

3mm diameter dowel

22mm (⅞in) between centres

15mm (⅝in) diameter bead

83mm (3¼in)

12mm (½in)

6mm (¼in)

73mm (2⅞in)

64mm (2½in)

70mm (2¾in)

6mm (¼in)

108mm (4¼in)

108mm (4¼in)

Top view of box

108mm (4¼in)

Fig.6

Chinese Towers Cutting List (All sizes are actual)				
No.	**Description**	**Material**	**Size (mm)**	**Size (inches)**
4 off	Box sides	Oak	108 x 70 x 6	4¼ x 2 3/4 x ¼
1 off	Box top	Oak	108 x 108 x 6	4¼ x 4¼ x ¼
1 off	Playing board	Oak	108 x 108 x 12	4¼ x 4¼ x ½
16 off	Dowel pegs	Ramin	73 x 4 dia.	2⅞ x ³⁄₁₆ dia.
64 off	Beads	Birch	16 dia.	⅝ dia.

Making the box

1 Refer to *figures 5 and 6*. The box that fits over the top of the game board is designed to be completely detachable so that all beads can be put into it at the start of the game.

2 Cut the four sides for length and width and after making box joints on the ends in the same way as the previous box, glue them together.

3 Before putting the lid on the box use the sides as a template to mark out the rebated area where the box

fits onto the game board. To do this, cut a piece of wood for the board slightly larger than required, place the sides of the box on top of it and mark around the inside edge with a pencil. This is so that when the board is made it will fit into the box accurately.

4 To make the box top, cut the same stock to approximately the correct size and glue it onto the top of the sides with the edges slightly overhanging. When the glue has set, plane the sides of the top so that they

Making the box for Chinese Towers.

are flush with the sides of the box, and at the same time clean up the outside of the box joints. The box is finished with two coats of golden oak brushing wax in the same way as the solitaire puzzle.

Game board

1 Refer to *figure 7*. The boundary of the playing area has already been marked out previously by drawing around the inside of the box sides. Onto this area is added 6mm (¼in) all around the boundary of the playing area for the rebate into which the sides of the box will eventually fit. Cut out the rectangle encompassed by these lines and form the rebate around the edge with a rebating plane or a router.

2 On the top of the game board draw a grid of lines to indicate where

Fig.7

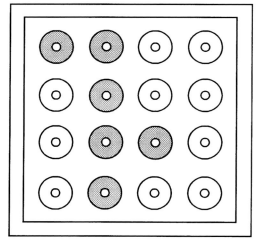

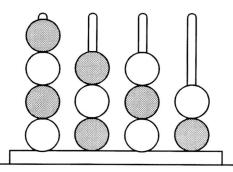

Make the holes vertical and to the correct depth.

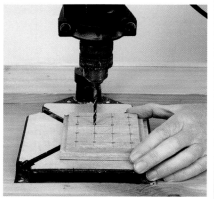

the holes are to be drilled for the lengths of dowel. Use a bradawl to pierce holes at the intersections of the lines to aid the location of the drilled holes. Use a 4mm (³/₁₆in) drill bit and make the holes vertical and to the correct depth.

③ From a length of 4mm (³/₁₆in) hardwood dowelling cut the pegs to size and using a pencil sharpener, chamfer the ends slightly. Because the oak board will be finished with golden oak brushing wax and the dowels will be left

unstained, the wax is applied to the board at this stage. Then glue the dowels into the holes.

Beads

Sixty-four wooden beads are required, 32 of one colour and 32 in a second contrasting colour. I chose 15mm (⅝in) diameter birchwood beads, one batch of which are clear varnished and the second group stained a deep brown colour. They were obtained from a craft shop that also sold bigger and smaller versions in a large variety of colours.

① The beads had small diameter holes pre-drilled as they were intended to be threaded for jewellery. These were re-drilled to a diameter of 5mm so that they would slide easily onto the 4mm (³/₁₆in) dowels. This can be a bit tricky, but I found that a pair of nutcrackers was ideal for holding them while drilling. ●

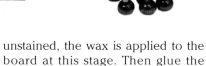

Gluing the dowels into the holes.

Since giving up his day job in the electronics pre-press industry, Dave Mackenzie now divides his time time between lecturing on woodworking and lecturing on graphic design, DTP and magazine journalism.
During the last 20 years he has had hundreds of magazine articles published on woodworking and DIY. Subjects have ranged from furniture design to kite making and much else in between. His first book, *Making Pine Furniture Projects* has recently been published by GMC Publications Ltd.
Dave Mackenzie is married with two children and enjoys painting and walking.

INDEX

INDEX

Titles available from
GMC PUBLICATIONS

BOOKS

WOODWORKING

40 More Woodworking Plans & Projects	*GMC Publications*	Making Little Boxes from Wood	*John Bennett*
Bird Boxes and Feeders for the Garden	*Dave Mackenzie*	Making Shaker Furniture	*Barry Jackson*
Complete Woodfinishing	*Ian Hosker*	Pine Furniture Projects for the Home	*Dave Mackenzie*
Electric Woodwork	*Jeremy Broun*	The Router and Furniture & Cabinetmaking	
Furniture & Cabinetmaking Projects	*GMC Publications*	Test Reports	*GMC Publications*
Furniture Projects	*Rod Wales*	Sharpening Pocket Reference Book	*Jim Kingshott*
Furniture Restoration (Practical Crafts)	*Kevin Jan Bonner*	Sharpening: The Complete Guide	*Jim Kingshott*
Furniture Restoration and Repair for Beginners	*Kevin Jan Bonner*	Space-Saving Furniture Projects	*Dave Mackenzie*
Green Woodwork	*Mike Abbott*	Stickmaking: A Complete Course	*Andrew Jones & Clive George*
The Incredible Router	*Jeremy Broun*	Veneering: A Complete Course	*Ian Hosker*
Making & Modifying Woodworking Tools	*Jim Kingshott*	Woodfinishing Handbook (Practical Crafts)	*Ian Hosker*
Making Chairs and Tables	*GMC Publications*	Woodworking Plans and Projects	*GMC Publications*
Making Fine Furniture	*Tom Darby*	The Workshop	*Jim Kingshott*

WOODTURNING

Adventures in Woodturning	*David Springett*	Practical Tips for Turners & Carvers	*GMC Publications*
Bert Marsh: Woodturner	*Bert Marsh*	Practical Tips for Woodturners	*GMC Publications*
Bill Jones' Notes from the Turning Shop	*Bill Jones*	Spindle Turning	*GMC Publications*
Bill Jones' Further Notes from the Turning Shop	*Bill Jones*	Turning Miniatures in Wood	*John Sainsbury*
Colouring Techniques for Woodturners	*Jan Sanders*	Turning Wooden Toys	*Terry Lawrence*
The Craftsman Woodturner	*Peter Child*	Understanding Woodturning	*Ann & Bob Phillips*
Decorative Techniques for Woodturners	*Hilary Bowen*	Useful Techniques for Woodturners	*GMC Publications*
Essential Tips for Woodturners	*GMC Publications*	Useful Woodturning Projects	*GMC Publications*
Faceplate Turning	*GMC Publications*	Woodturning: A Foundation Course	*Keith Rowley*
Fun at the Lathe	*R.C. Bell*	Woodturning: A Source Book of Shapes	*John Hunnex*
Illustrated Woodturning Techniques	*John Hunnex*	Woodturning Jewellery	*Hilary Bowen*
Intermediate Woodturning Projects	*GMC Publications*	Woodturning Masterclass	*Tony Boase*
Keith Rowley's Woodturning Projects	*Keith Rowley*	Woodturning Techniques	*GMC Publications*
Make Money from Woodturning	*Ann & Bob Phillips*	Woodturning Tools & Equipment	
Multi-Centre Woodturning	*Ray Hopper*	Test Reports	*GMC Publications*
Pleasure and Profit from Woodturning	*Reg Sherwin*	Woodturning Wizardry	*David Springett*

WOODCARVING

The Art of the Woodcarver	*GMC Publications*	Understanding Woodcarving in the Round	*GMC Publications*
Carving Birds & Beasts	*GMC Publications*	Useful Techniques for Woodcarvers	*GMC Publications*
Carving on Turning	*Chris Pye*	Wildfowl Carving - Volume 1	*Jim Pearce*
Carving Realistic Birds	*David Tippey*	Wildfowl Carving - Volume 2	*Jim Pearce*
Decorative Woodcarving	*Jeremy Williams*	The Woodcarvers	*GMC Publications*
Essential Tips for Woodcarvers	*GMC Publications*	Woodcarving: A Complete Course	*Ron Butterfield*
Essential Woodcarving Techniques	*Dick Onians*	Woodcarving: A Foundation Course	*Zoë Gertner*
Lettercarving in Wood: A Practical Course	*Chris Pye*	Woodcarving for Beginners	*GMC Publications*
Practical Tips for Turners & Carvers	*GMC Publications*	Woodcarving Tools & Equipment	
Relief Carving in Wood: A Practical Introduction	*Chris Pye*	Test Reports	*GMC Publications*
Understanding Woodcarving	*GMC Publications*	Woodcarving Tools, Materials & Equipment	*Chris Pye*

UPHOLSTERY

Seat Weaving (Practical Crafts)	*Ricky Holdstock*	Upholstery Restoration	*David James*
Upholsterer's Pocket Reference Book	*David James*	Upholstery Techniques & Projects	*David James*
Upholstery: A Complete Course	*David James*		

TOYMAKING

Designing & Making Wooden Toys	*Terry Kelly*	Restoring Rocking Horses	*Clive Green & Anthony Dew*
Fun to Make Wooden Toys & Games	*Jeff & Jennie Loader*	Scrollsaw Toy Projects	*Ivor Carlyle*
Making Board, Peg & Dice Games	*Jeff & Jennie Loader*	Wooden Toy Projects	*GMC Publications*
Making Wooden Toys & Games	*Jeff & Jennie Loader*		

DOLLS' HOUSES AND MINIATURES

Architecture for Dolls' Houses	*Joyce Percival*	Making Period Dolls' House Accessories	*Andrea Barham*
Beginners' Guide to the Dolls' House Hobby	*Jean Nisbett*	Making Period Dolls' House Furniture	*Derek & Sheila Rowbottom*
The Complete Dolls' House Book	*Jean Nisbett*	Making Tudor Dolls' Houses	*Derek Rowbottom*
Dolls' House Accessories, Fixtures and Fittings	*Andrea Barham*	Making Unusual Miniatures	*Graham Spalding*
Dolls' House Bathrooms: Lots of Little Loos	*Patricia King*	Making Victorian Dolls' House Furniture	*Patricia King*
Easy to Make Dolls' House Accessories	*Andrea Barham*	Miniature Bobbin Lace	*Roz Snowden*
Make Your Own Dolls' House Furniture	*Maurice Harper*	Miniature Embroidery for the Victorian Dolls' House	*Pamela Warner*
Making Dolls' House Furniture	*Patricia King*	Miniature Needlepoint Carpets	*Janet Granger*
Making Georgian Dolls' Houses	*Derek Rowbottom*	The Secrets of the Dolls' House Makers	*Jean Nisbett*
Making Miniature Oriental Rugs & Carpets	*Meik & Ian McNaughton*		

CRAFTS

American Patchwork Designs in Needlepoint	*Melanie Tacon*	Embroidery Tips & Hints	*Harold Hayes*
A Beginners' Guide to Rubber Stamping	*Brenda Hunt*	An Introduction to Crewel Embroidery	*Mave Glenny*
Celtic Knotwork Designs	*Sheila Sturrock*	Making Character Bears	*Valerie Tyler*
Collage from Seeds, Leaves and Flowers	*Joan Carver*	Making Greetings Cards for Beginners	*Pat Sutherland*
Complete Pyrography	*Stephen Poole*	Making Knitwear Fit	*Pat Ashforth & Steve Plummer*
Creating Knitwear Designs	*Pat Ashforth & Steve Plummer*	Needlepoint: A Foundation Course	*Sandra Hardy*
Creative Embroidery Techniques		Pyrography Handbook (Practical Crafts)	*Stephen Poole*
Using Colour Through Gold	*Daphne J. Ashby & Jackie Woolsey*	Tassel Making for Beginners	*Enid Taylor*
Cross Stitch Kitchen Projects	*Janet Granger*	Tatting Collage	*Lindsay Rogers*
Cross Stitch on Colour	*Sheena Rogers*	Temari: A Traditional Japanese Embroidery Technique	*Margaret Ludlow*

THE HOME

Home Ownership: Buying and Maintaining	*Nicholas Snelling*	Security for the Householder: Fitting Locks and Other Devices	*E. Phillips*

VIDEOS

Drop-in and Pinstuffed Seats	*David James*	Twists and Advanced Turning	*Dennis White*
Stuffover Upholstery	*David James*	Sharpening the Professional Way	*Jim Kingshott*
Elliptical Turning	*David Springett*	Sharpening Turning & Carving Tools	*Jim Kingshott*
Woodturning Wizardry	*David Springett*	Bowl Turning	*John Jordan*
Turning Between Centres: The Basics	*Dennis White*	Hollow Turning	*John Jordan*
Turning Bowls	*Dennis White*	Woodturning: A Foundation Course	*Keith Rowley*
Boxes, Goblets and Screw Threads	*Dennis White*	Carving a Figure: The Female Form	*Ray Gonzalez*
Novelties and Projects	*Dennis White*	The Router: A Beginner's Guide	*Alan Goodsell*
Classic Profiles	*Dennis White*	The Scroll Saw: A Beginner's Guide	*John Burke*

MAGAZINES

**Woodturning • Woodcarving • Furniture & Cabinetmaking • The Router
The Dolls' House Magazine • Creative Crafts for the Home • BusinessMatters**

The above represents a full list of all titles currently published or scheduled to be published.
All are available direct from the Publishers or through bookshops, newsagents and specialist retailers.
To place an order, or to obtain a complete catalogue, contact:

GMC Publications,
166 High Street, Lewes, East Sussex BN7 1XU, United Kingdom Tel: 01273 488005 Fax: 01273 478606

Orders by credit card are accepted

10|00